The Young Paul Robeson

To Nicole Du Pree
and Vera Baker
best wishes,
Lloyd L Brown
7/17/96

The Young Paul Robeson

"On My Journey Now"

by Lloyd L. Brown

Westview Press
A Member of Perseus Books, L.L.C.

Frontispiece: Paul Robeson as a Rutgers junior (courtesy of Special Collections and Archives, Rutgers University)

Published in 1997 in the United States of America by Westview Press, 5500 Central Avenue, Boulder, Colorado, 80301-2877, and in the United Kingdom by Westview Press, 12 Hid's Copse Road, Cumnor Hill, Oxford OX2 9JJ

Library of Congress Cataloging-in-Publication Data
Brown, Lloyd L. (Lloyd Louis), 1913–
    The young Paul Robeson : "on my journey now" / Lloyd L. Brown
        p.   cm.
    Includes index.
    ISBN 0-8133-3178-1   ISBN 0-8133-3177-3 (pbk)
    1. Robeson, Paul, 1898–1976—Childhood and youth.   2. Singers—
United States—Biography.   3. Actors—United States—Biography.
4. Afro-Americans—Biography.   I. Title.
E185.97.R63B76   1997
782´.0092—dc20
[B]   96-24715
                                                                                        CIP

Design by Jane Raese

10   9   8   7   6   5   4

To Holly and Heather

Contents

Photographs

Preface

Now here I stand at Paul Robeson's grave. "Paul," I say, looking down at his name on the bronze marker, "was there ever a more reluctant subject for a biography than you?" Like a flash I think of the rejoinder that Paul could have made: "And was there ever a more reluctant biographer than you were, Lloyd?" We would have shared a laugh at that exchange, coming nearly forty years after he first asked me to assist him in writing his autobiography.

The raised lettering on the plaque, which is set flush with the ground on the edge of this pathway, reads as follows:

PAUL ROBESON
APRIL 9, 1898   JAN. 23, 1976
"THE ARTIST MUST ELECT TO FIGHT
FOR FREEDOM OR SLAVERY. I
HAVE MADE MY CHOICE. I HAD
NO ALTERNATIVE."

The quotation is from a 1937 speech by Robeson in London, where the world-famous concert singer and actor had plunged into the growing movement against fascism.[1] "Well, Paul," I say, "you never did write an autobiography, but as it turned out you did write your own epitaph, and no one could have done it better."

My wife, Lily, who has been busy placing on Lawrence Brown's grave his share of the flowers she brought, now joins me and joshingly asks if I am still talking to Paul. I have a joke of my own for a comeback. "What about Larry?" I say. "Was he disappointed that you didn't bring him some imported flowers this time?" (Lawrence Brown, who prided himself on being a connoisseur of the finer things of life, had been delighted that Lily had brought him a bouquet of French-grown mimosa blossoms the last time we visited him in Harlem Hospital. It was Christmas Eve, the night before he died.)

Because he had no living relatives, I had kept Brown's ashes for future burial in whatever cemetery would be chosen for Robeson's eventual interment. For the bronze marker on Brown's grave I chose some words by Paul for that epitaph as well. The selected phrase came from a message Robeson had sent to the memorial meeting in Harlem that marked the passing of his longtime coworker. That tablet reads:

LAWRENCE BROWN

1893   1972

HIS MUSIC

WILL NEVER DIE

In his tape-recorded message to that gathering in St. Martin's Episcopal Church, Paul, after expressing deep regret that ill health prevented his attendance, noted that "Larry was my close friend and partner for forty years."[2]

Indeed, at the beginning of their careers as singer and accompanist, Robeson and Brown were equal partners, and their manager was Eslanda Goode Robeson. She was Mrs. Paul Robeson then, and she would triumphantly remain Mrs. Paul Robeson for the rest of her life. Essie, as Paul's wife was always known, was largely responsible for pushing and pulling her reluctant spouse to become a professional performer, first as an actor and then as a singer. Brown, who was five years older than Robeson, had already established himself as a published composer and arranger and had served for several years as accompanist for Roland Hayes, the noted black tenor.

Essie was the first of the three to die, and her ashes were kept for burial beside her husband's grave. And so we gaze upon a third bronze plaque, next to Paul's, which is inscribed:

ESLANDA GOODE ROBESON

DEC. 15, 1896   DEC. 13, 1965

Her name, two dates, and nothing else on the memorial installed by her son.

To my surprise I feel a surge of pity for Essie, though never once had I felt even a twinge of sympathy for her during all the years I knew her. That lack of sympathy was not because our friendship was always merely diplomatic, which it certainly was. The fact is, Essie was simply not a person to evoke much sympathy from anyone. To hear her talk, everything was always all right with her—"perfectly *mah*velous," she would say, using the British upper-class accent she adopted during the Robesons' years in London.

Looking down now at the dates that show Essie died just two days before her sixty-ninth birthday, Lily and I recall that not even the imminence of death could make her drop that pose of jaunty self-satisfaction. On our last visit to her in the hospital, a couple of days before the cancer finally won its ten-year fight to kill her, Essie told us that she would have to postpone her birthday party, to which she had invited us. It seemed that the silly doctors thought some more tests were necessary before she could leave, which was really quite ridiculous since she felt ever so much better now—and she flashed her practiced smile to prove it. "So *there*," she said, dismissing us by her tone. "We're still going to have a perfectly *mah*velous party!" At the door I glanced back for a farewell look. Her aristocratic manner was heightened now by the way her gray hair was braided around her head like a tiara, and the unwavering smile told the world that Mrs. Paul Robeson still had it made.

So it must be said: Essie's courage and determination were monumental. One word, "Indomitable," could be her epitaph.

Trying to think of some other words to sum up a personality that often seemed as hard and cold and inflexible as this metal plaque, my sympathy, like a compass needle swinging back to its true position, now returns to Paul. An ambitious wife who pushes and pulls her spouse into a career not of his choosing is bound to become a nag, and it was that aspect of their relationship that first came to my attention.

In boyhood I had of course heard about the legendary football hero "Robeson of Rutgers"—incredible as it seems nowadays, famous black athletes in the United States could then be counted on the fingers of one hand—but I had never heard of Essie until the time, just before World War II, that Lily and I first attended a Robeson concert. On his program that evening at Pittsburgh's Syria Mosque was the *Show Boat* song "I Still Suits Me," in which a husband mimics the nagging complaints of his wife and brazenly defies her efforts to make him do as she wishes. At one point in his rendition, which seemed to delight the singer as much as the audience, Lawrence Brown's piano paused, permitting Paul to look offstage and say in a loud whisper that reached us in the balcony, "Watch out, Essie!" That byplay was good for a laugh at every performance until Paul dropped the song from his repertoire. "The women progressives—they got after me about it," Paul once told me with a mischievous grin, referring to the left-wing forerunners of the later women's liberation movement.

Many of Paul's friends from his early years were certain that Essie was responsible for her husband's later radical ideas and activities. Her dominating personality made it seem logical that she who had directed the young graduate of Columbia Law School away from the practice of law and toward a career as an actor must have guided his political orientation as well. Then too, the ill will that most of Paul's friends and family had for Essie made them eager to blame her for the seemingly inexplicable transformation of the good-hearted and easygoing young Paul they admired into the militant activist he had become. It was Essie's malignant influence, some of them confided to my tape recorder, that had misled the popular All-American hero to become denounced as a so-called un-American.

As a matter of fact, Essie could not be blamed or credited (depending on one's viewpoint) for Paul's development as an uncompromising black militant and anti-imperialist. "I have made my choice" are the words on his plaque, and what could be clearer than that? And when he went on to say, "I had no alternative," the guiding force behind that imperative was not his wife but his father: not Eslanda Goode Robeson but the Reverend William Drew Robeson.

Now Lily and I go back to our car for the short drive home on the Saw Mill River Parkway. It is fewer than twenty miles from Ferncliff Cemetery at Hartsdale to our Manhattan neighborhood—the same neighborhood where Paul and Essie had their last home in New York, a brownstone house at 16 Jumel Terrace.

Ferncliff is located in Westchester County, New York, and so is the city of Peekskill that was mentioned in Robeson's foreword to his book, *Here I Stand.* He recalled having "heard, only a few miles away, at Peekskill, the baying of the lynch-mob, the cries for my life from hate-twisted mouths."[3] Paul's choice of what to fight for had brought him to that crucial confrontation, and I'm sure he would be pleased that his defiant epitaph speaks to posterity from this particular location.

I am grateful to my fellow traveler for suggesting that we make this pilgrimage today, on Paul's birthday. Some people visit the graves of those they loved, whereas others, no less devoted in memory, never go unless someone induces them to do so. Paul Robeson belonged to that second category. "I loved him like no one else in all the world," he wrote of his father,[4] whose funeral he attended in 1918; but I believe that the only time he visited his father's grave was more than thirty years later.

I was with him on that occasion, in the fall of 1952, when we went to Princeton, New Jersey, on a field trip for the autobiography on which I was to assist him. One of his friends from his boyhood days in that town, who had volunteered to show us around, asked Paul if he would like to visit his parents' graves in the cemetery across the street from the church Paul's father had pastored for many years. Paul, of course, had to say yes.

When the caretaker took us to the graves, Paul was plainly embarrassed as we saw what he must have known: His parents' adjoining graves were the only ones without headstones. Paul's mother, Maria Louisa, had been interred there fourteen years before her husband's death, and it was understood that eventually her grave would share a common monument with his.

After we had stood there for a few respectful minutes and were walking away, I heard Paul say, more to himself than to me, that he must talk to Ben about this. Ben was his older brother, the Reverend Benjamin C. Robeson, who had been put in charge of clearing out his father's parsonage and seeing to the erection of a gravestone. Alas for history, Ben performed his first task all too well: When he cleared out the house, he discarded every scrap of his parents' papers. As for the second task, he never installed the monument. The two surviving sons of the senior Reverend Robeson evidently had little regard for such things as graves and headstones, and I doubt that Paul ever bothered to remind Ben about his unfinished responsibility.

Paul was a deeply spiritual man, utterly unconcerned with material things. But intangibles—principles and ideals—how he clung to them! My close association with him continued until the end of his days, and I saw how permanently fixed in his makeup was the influence of his father. As a young man of twenty-one, Paul had resolved to make his life a memorial to the man he called "Pop"; when he publicly uttered that vow, those who heard him probably thought the earnest-looking young man, erect and solemn in his high, starched collar, was merely voicing a sentimental tribute to Reverend Robeson, who had died the year before.

Paul's statement was made in New Brunswick, New Jersey, on the eve of his graduation from Rutgers University in 1919, when some leading citizens of the city gave a banquet in his honor. The local newspaper, reporting the event under the heading "Paul Robeson Gets Purse as Token of Esteem," noted that the speakers had expressed "their regrets at the departure of one so well-loved and respected" and that "Mr. Robeson in reply said he hoped his life work would be a memorial to his father's training and that his work was not for his own self but that he might help the race to a higher life."[5]

Twenty-four years after Paul and I visited those unmarked graves in Princeton, a large granite tombstone was erected there by Marian Robeson Forsythe, Paul's sister, who took care of her invalid brother for the last ten years of his life. Though in poor health herself, Marian, who was several years older than her brother, told me about a deal she had made with God: He was to keep her going as long as Paul needed her. Perhaps as a bonus for her loving devotion and for the sweetness of her personality, which blessed everyone who knew her, Marian was given an extra year of life after Paul was gone.

When Paul wrote that Lawrence Brown's music will never die, he was referring to his partner's work in collecting, arranging, publishing, and popularizing many of the Negro spirituals that had come down solely in oral form from those "black and unknown bards" who created this now world-acclaimed body of folk songs. The first phonograph recordings of Robeson and Brown were made at the Victor Talking Machine Company in Camden, New Jersey, where they recorded on wax such spirituals as "Bye and Bye," "Steal Away," "On My Journey Now," and "Joshua Fit the Battle of Jericho."

During the so-called Fearful Fifties, Robeson's attorney and friends were concerned that the record companies, which had ceased to produce any Robeson recordings, might be pressured to destroy the original master recordings he had made. Many terrible things like that were done by J. Edgar Hoover's minions in the McCarthy period, when numerous efforts were made to blot out all sight and sound of Paul Robeson and to deny even the listing of his name in any creditable manner. However, his friends' fears about the recordings were groundless, and as the Red Scare abated many were reissued.

So, this evening when Lily and I get home we can listen to the velvety baritone of the young Paul Robeson (later he would be a bass-baritone) and try to hold back the tears as his artistry evokes the compassion his enslaved forebears expressed in their tender sorrow song, "Were You There?" And we will be assured that although nobody knows the trouble they've seen, bye and bye they're gonna lay down their heavy load and study war no more.

As we drink a birthday toast to the memory of Paul, who "broke our hearts with beauty" and whose art was such a mighty weapon in the liberation struggle, we can recall some lines he liked from "Let the Rail Splitter Awake" by Pablo Neruda. During his blacklisted years, Robeson would often end a concert or speech by reciting these words of the poem written when Neruda, a former Chilean senator, had been exiled by the right-wing government of his homeland:

> *Let none think of me.*
> *Let us think of the entire earth*
> *and pound the table with love.*
> *I don't want blood again*
> *to saturate bread, beans, music.*
> *I wish they would come with me:*
> *the miner, the little girl,*
> *the lawyer, the seaman,*
> *the doll-maker,*
> *to go into a movie and come out*
> *to drink the reddest wine.*
> *I did not come here to solve anything.*
> *I came here to sing*
> *and for you to sing with me.*[6]

Lloyd L. Brown
New York
April 9, 1996

Acknowledgments

Of the many persons who encouraged and assisted the author, there are three to be mentioned first. They are Paul Robeson, of course; and his sister, Marian Forsythe; and Lily Brown, my wife and partner for fifty-nine years and a devoted fellow-researcher for this book.

Among others who deserve special mention—

Angus Cameron, the distinguished book editor, who years ago was patiently encouraging to me in what must have been the most prolonged author's work-in-progress he ever encountered, offered creative suggestions for the present book that were of great value.

Sender Garlin, who in his early nineties must be the dean of American labor journalists, was a keen-eyed reader of the manuscript, calling my attention to various errors therein and—bless him—helping me find a publisher who would share his warm assessment of this work.

Sterling Stuckey, professor of history and religious studies at the University of California at Riverside, whose perceptive studies of Robeson have been included in several of his books, encouraged my own work over a span of years.

Dean Birkenkamp, formerly chief editor at Westview Press, who happily was conversant with the relevant literature, made several suggestions of major importance that were gratefully accepted.

In large ways or small, the following persons were helpful to me as a Robeson biographer, and their assistance is hereby thankfully acknowledged. However, the responsibility for the rendering of this story and for any errors in the text is, of course, mine alone. (The names of those interviewed on tape are given in italics.)

Walter Abel, Joseph O. Andrews, Herbert Aptheker, *Dame Peggy Ashcroft,* Frank E. Barnes, Louise Berman, Richard O. Boyer, *J. Douglas Brown, Lawrence B. Brown,* Linda L. Brown, Louis Burnham, Barba-Del Campbell, *May E. Chinn, M.D.,* Earle Conover, Marvel Cooke, Benjamin J. Davis Jr., Freda Diamond, Stanley Douglas, *Bess Eitingon, William A.*

THE YOUNG PAUL ROBESON

Feitner, Jane Fisher, Pearl Fisher, Joseph H. Filner, Jimmie Fleming, John Hope Franklin, Muriel Freeman, *Margaret (Potter) Gibbons,* Nina Goodman, Benjamin F. Gordon, Gil Green, George Gregory, *Stella Bloch Hanau, M. Harold Higgins,* Christine Moore Howell, W. Alphaeus Hunton, Dorothy Hunton, Harrison Johnson, George A. Kuyper, *Patti Light,* Carrie Lloyd, Edward Magdol, Francis Marion Manning, Berdella (Bert) McGee, Betty Millard, Warren Moore, George B. Murphy Jr., *Alfred A. Neuschaefer,* Judith B. Nichols, William L. Patterson, *Frederick (Fritz) Pollard, Kenneth M. Rendall, Milton J. Rettenberg,* Virginia Bustill Smith Rhetta, Paul D. Roberson, Vernon Roberson, Harry J. Rockafeller, Clara Rockmore, Helen Rosen, Samuel Rosen, *G. Foster Sanford Jr.,* Anatol I. Schlosser, Pete Seeger, Marie Seton, Dorothy Sterling, J. Harold Thomson, *Dame Sybil Thorndike,* Arthur K. Van Fleet, Mary D. Walden, Samuel Woldin, Louise Dahl Wolfe.

Information was also obtained at the following institutions:

Akademie der Künste der DDR, Paul Robeson Archiv
Boston Public Library
Chester County Historical Society, Library and Museum
Library of Congress
Martin County Courthouse, Williamston, N.C.
National Archives
Archives and History Bureau, New Jersey State Library
New York Public Library
Princeton University Library
Research and Archives, Historical Society of Princeton
Rutgers University Archives
State Archives, Raleigh, North Carolina
Vail Memorial Library, Lincoln University

L.L.B.

PART ONE

I Got a Home in-a That Rock

Rich man Dives, he lived so well,
When he died he found a home in Hell,
He had no home in-a that rock,
Don't you see.

—from a Negro spiritual composed by slaves and sung
by Paul Robeson at his first New York concert, April 19, 1925

1

An African American

THERE WAS ALWAYS A LARGENESS about Paul Robeson. Even before he entered public life to become world famous as an actor, concert singer, and leader in militant movements for black liberation and peace, Robeson was seen by his college associates as a man of many parts, all of them exemplary. That assessment of the man—the first overall appraisal of him to be published—appeared when he graduated from college in 1919 at the age of twenty-one. An editorial farewell to him in the Rutgers student magazine asserted that "this negro, unheralded and unknown" when he entered the school, had in his four years "made a name and a record equalled by none." He had had "an athletic career without equal," had been "each year an honor man" in his studies, and was a "speaker of deep thought and marvelous ability [who] won the class oratorical prize four years in succession." Noting that "one may combine physical and mental ability and still lack the most important element in one's character, moral stamina," the editorial asserted that in this respect Robeson had proved "he was a man through and through"; and the hope was expressed that "Rutgers never forget this noble son."[1]

Throughout his career the largeness of Paul Robeson was cited by many. In Robeson's middle years, the noted black scholar Mary McLeod Bethune would greet him as "the tallest tree in our forest," and many white Americans at that time saw him as the embodiment of the Whitmanesque concept: "I am large, I contain multitudes." In a later decade his numerous enemies and detractors also testified to his stature by making him a central symbol of the enormous danger they saw as threatening them at home and abroad. The *Saturday Evening Post,* most widely circulated American magazine at the time, saw Robeson as "a Soviet weapon in the war for the minds of the world's colored peoples, and especially for the Red capture of Africa."² And late in Robeson's life the Nobel prize-winning poet Pablo Neruda would endow him with a cosmic universality in an ode composed in his honor: "You have been the voice of man,/the song of the germinating earth,/and the movement of nature."³

This many-sided man, who came to identify himself with people of many different nationalities and cultures, always saw himself as a product of his own people. The simple statement "I am a Negro" was the opening sentence of one of his first published articles,⁴ and it was also the first sentence of his book, *Here I Stand*, written twenty-five years later. That key element of his self-definition is missing from this dictionary definition: "Robeson, Paul (rōb' s'n, rō' bi-s'n), 1898–   ; American singer and actor."⁵ Had Robeson (he and his family used the first pronunciation given) been merely an American and not an African American, his whole story would have been utterly different. But central to everything about him as an artist and citizen was the fact that he was of that one-tenth of the American people who are of African descent and who, over their nearly 400-year history in this country, have variously termed themselves "colored," "Negro," "black," "Afro-American," or "African-American."*

The early article mentioned above, which was written by Robeson in 1934 and entitled "I Want to Be African," reflected his quest for the lost cultural heritage. "Like most of Africa's children in America," he later recalled, "I had known little about the land of our fathers [until] in England I came to know many Africans."⁶ That acquaintanceship occurred in London when he was in his thirties and began an extensive study of African languages and cultures. Robeson came to believe that his roots were in West Africa, and when he found in the language of that region "a kinship of rhythm and intonation with the Negro-English dialect which I heard spoken around me as a child," it was, he wrote, "like a homecoming."⁷

Even before he "discovered Africa in London," as he put it, Robeson had been pleased that from the outset of his stage career critics and interviewers had described him as being strikingly African in appearance—"classically African," as one British writer noted, "with broad flaring nostrils, full lips and dark skin."⁸ Then, too, his statuesque bearing, which was

---

* In conversation, speeches, and writings, Paul Robeson made use of all of these terms, though his preference was for "Negro," which in his young manhood in Harlem had become the designation favored by those who asserted pride in their race. In the 1960s, after his retirement, the term "black" became the choice of a new generation that had discovered—again—that "black is beautiful" and did not know that the word "black" is more Aryan than its Latinate synonym, "Negro."

often described as "noble," evoked journalistic comments that likened him to some African chief. Thus, in his twenties the fledgling black actor was said to have the "ineffable dignity of some Somali chieftain."[9]

Robeson's first biographer—his wife, Eslanda Goode Robeson—went beyond such comparisons when, in writing about her husband's father, William D. Robeson, she asserted that when he was a youth in slavery, "It was said by the old blacks in Martin County that 'W. D.' resembled in many ways his Bantu ancestors."[10] That account, based upon invented hearsay, was embellished by Robeson's second biographer, Shirley Graham, who conjured up a "wrinkled old voodoo woman" to whisper into William Robeson's ear about his "mighty" Bantu forebears. "Ah know yo', boy," she told him. "Ah know yo' great-gran'sire in Af'ica. No mahn could make a slave o' he, no mahn could break he will, o' ben' he back!"[11]

A later biographer, the historian Martin Bauml Duberman, revised those accounts to say that it was actually Robeson's mother, Maria Louisa Bustill, who was descended from the "African Bantu people" and that Paul Robeson's father traced his roots back to "the Ibo of Nigeria."[12] However, as we shall see, nothing is known of any specific African connection with either side of Robeson's family. Under chattel slavery, when those held in bondage usually did not know even the date of their own birth, the Robesons and the Bustills—like almost all the others—could not have had any knowledge of their ancestral forebears.

Though accounts of Robeson's alleged descent from African royalty are not faithful to fact, they are quite faithful to the "noble savage" stereotype in American fiction that often revealed that admirable nonwhite characters were descended from royal "native" ancestry. Robeson's great pride in his father and in the African heritage he claimed for all black Americans was based upon no such fanciful pretensions. Reacting with amusement to assertions by some African Americans that their ancestors in Africa had been kings and queens, Robeson once remarked to this writer, "Our people especially should know better than that. After all, who were the folks who did the work?"

Though we know nothing of Robeson's great-great-grandsires in Africa, a considerable record does exist concerning an American-born great-great-grandfather and his descendants. That documentary record reveals that Paul Robeson, who was often said to be a composite man in other respects, was indeed a veritable composite of the African American. Characteristically that ethnic group is an admixture of three so-called races: black African, "red" Native American, and white European; and Robeson's family is typical of that development.

A composite African American would also be, as Robeson was, a product of the two branches of black America that developed historically from the enslaved Africans brought to the English colonies in the New World beginning in 1619. The main branch, by far the most numerous, was in the South, where for 150 years they toiled on the plantations—until slavery was abolished after the Civil War. The much smaller number who made up the Northern branch, most of them household servants, gained their emancipation much earlier, in some instances prior to the American Revolution, as was the case with the first of Robeson's known forebears on his mother's side.*

Paul Robeson's father, William, a fugitive slave, came from the Southern branch of black America—tillers of the soil who, though tutored only by the lash, still managed to produce the most seminal cultural contribution made by any ethnic group in this country, namely, the Negro spirituals. From the ranks of the Southern slaves came such heroic figures as Denmark Vesey and Nat Turner, leaders of slave revolts, and fugitives who became abolitionist leaders: Frederick Douglass, Harriet Tubman, William Wells Brown, Henry Highland Garnet, and many others. Robeson's mother, Maria Louisa Bustill, was descended from the Northern branch, which under conditions of quasi-freedom in urban centers had produced the first African American writers, clergymen, teachers, physicians, and businessmen and established the first black-controlled churches, benevolent associations, schools, and newspapers. From their ranks came notable figures in the antislavery struggle: David Walker, a free North Carolinian who moved North; James Forten; Robert Purvis; Alexander Crummell; Charles Remond; Martin Delany; and numerous others, including several of Robeson's maternal forebears.

Thus the marriage of Paul Robeson's parents in 1878—twenty years before his birth—united two persons who were, as will be shown, archetypically representative of the two main branches of the African American people.

---

* See Appendix A: "The Proud Bustills."

2

William Robeson:
A Star to Follow

*W*HEN AT THE AGE OF SIXTY Paul Robeson undertook to give some answers to a black newspaper reporter's question, "Who, what, and why is Paul Robeson?" he began by referring to "the man, now forty years dead, who more than anyone else influenced my life—my father, Reverend William Drew Robeson."[1] The persistence of that decisive influence was evident in a newspaper column Robeson wrote in 1952 wherein he mused: "'What would Pop think?' I often stop and ask the stars, the winds. I often stretch out my arm as I used to, to put it around Pop's shoulder and ask, 'How'm I doin', Pop?'"[2]

The circumstances that caused the son throughout his life to measure himself by his father's standards will be examined later, but here it might be noted that in private conversation as well as in public writings and speeches Robeson invariably identified himself with his African American background solely in terms of his father and his father's people in the South.* A typical example was the explanation he gave to a convention of black trade unionists as to why, though he had "attained some status and acclaim as an artist," he nevertheless devoted time and energy to the concerns of working men and women. "I have simply tried never to forget the soil from which I spring," he said. "Never to forget the rich but abused

---

* Perhaps the only exception to that practice was in Robeson's book, *Here I Stand*, where he cited the Bustill side of his family in arguing that African Americans were second to none in having a rightful claim to the American heritage.

7

earth in the eastern coast of North Carolina where my father—not my grandfather—was a slave; and where today many of my cousins and other relatives still live in poverty and second-class citizenship."[3]

∽ ∽ ∽

Robersonville, North Carolina, was named for George O. Robason, Henry D. Roberson, and William W. Roberson,[4] who were the heads of three branches of a slaveholding family in Martin County, which is located on the eastern coastal plain of that state. It was from that family that the surname of the black Robesons was derived. The Robersons were early settlers in North Carolina, and over the generations members of that numerous family spelled their name also as "Robason," "Robuson," "Robson," or "Robeson," which is the name of a county in another part of the state.*

It is not known how far back the black Robeson line extends in this country—whether any of Robeson's forebears were among the 100,783 slaves who made up one-fourth of North Carolina's population in 1790 (the first Federal census) or if they were brought from Africa later. The first known members of the Southern branch of Paul Robeson's family were his grandparents, Benjamin and Sabra, though the record about them is scant. No reference to Benjamin, who was born in 1820, was found in the few Roberson wills that survived a fire at the Martin County courthouse.

In 1828 Henry Robason (the then current spelling) left to his grandchildren "my Negro man George and also my Negro man David for the purpose of raising and supporting them . . . and also my three horses for the same use." As was the custom, he also directed that a black human being would be disposed of to leave the deceased's affairs in proper order: "I leave my Negro woman Matilda to be sold to pay for my debts and funeral expenses."[5] "My friend James Congleton," named in the will as an executor, may be significant in regard to Benjamin, who after Emancipation adopted "Congleton" as his surname. (Paul Robeson once recalled hearing his father say that his own father, Benjamin, had taken the name from a certain Congleton who in some way had helped the freedman to acquire some land.)

---

* Regardless of spelling, the North Carolina pronunciation of the name is "Rôb-a-s'n" or "Rôb-s'n." In Martin County the spelling has been standardized as "Roberson": The 1971 telephone book for Robersonville and adjacent localities listed no fewer than 157 subscribers named Roberson. None of the previously used variant spellings appeared.

Another Robason will may have referred to Benjamin's wife,* Sabra (pronounced "Say-bra" or, colloquially, "Say-bree"), who was born in 1825. In that will William Robason in 1845 bequeathed to his son, George O. Robason, "One Negro Boy named Arden, One Cow & Calf [and] One Feather Bed"; and among other human-property bequests he left to his daughter Caroline "One Negro Girl named Sabry during her [Caroline's] natural life and then to her children."[6] If "Sabry" was, as is likely, the Sabra who was mother to William Robeson, Paul's father, that will as far as she was concerned was nullified twenty years later when the Thirteenth Amendment outlawed chattel slavery.

Sabra's son, William, who knew his birthday as July 27, 1845, must have been counted in the Federal Census of 1850, which was taken shortly after his fifth birthday. At that time the Martin County population of 8,300 included 3,500 black slaves and 320 black persons who were listed as "free." (Though the latter had somehow emancipated themselves from chattel bondage, they were nevertheless tethered by a state law prohibiting them from traveling beyond the borders of the counties that adjoined the county where they lived.)[7] Most of the white Robasons listed were poor farmers and laborers, but ten families of that name were shown to be slaveowners, holding from one to thirteen slaves; this was considerably fewer than the number owned by the richest men in the county, who held as many as ninety-four.

The slaves were listed separately, as property of their owners, and were identified not by name but only as to age and sex. As it happened, there were four male slaves of about William's age owned variously by three Robason slaveholders—Sarah, Henry, and William, and so it cannot be determined which of the four boys listed was the one who nearly a half century later would become Paul Robeson's father.

In the census taken a decade later, thirteen Robason families owned slaves and this time six of them had a young male slave around William's age. However, from other evidence it seems probable that the owner from whom young William would soon emancipate himself was George O. Robason, one of the three men for whom Robersonville was later named, and whose grandson would one day encounter Paul Robeson in New York.

---

* Though slaves could not be legally married, the union of Benjamin and Sabra was a stable relationship that lasted more than forty years.

If a slave could not get his name into the census record, he could, as many did, get his name into print by running away, as seen by the following advertisement that appeared in 1856 in a Martin County newspaper ironically named *The Democratic Banner:*

$25 REWARD

Runaway from the subscriber, on the 24th of July, my boy LONDON, who was formerly owned by S. H. McRae, of Washington county.

He is about 20 years old, 5 feet 10 inches high, color medium, handsome and of good address. The above reward will be given for the apprehension and safe delivery, or safe confinement in Jail where I can find him.

T. C. HYMAN[8]

Had he seen that notice it would have meant nothing to William, who was then eleven and could not read a word. But he who cannot read still can run, and when William got the chance he also lit out on the road to freedom. No advertisement about him would appear, however, because when he ran away he was part of a mass movement.

In later life William, who learned to read not only English but also Latin and Greek, may have written an account of when and how he escaped from bondage, but unfortunately none of his correspondence, writings, or sermons have been preserved; and he did not tell any details of the story to his children. In Eslanda Robeson's book, William was said to have become a fugitive in 1860, when he was fifteen; and all other writers on the subject, including Paul Robeson, used that data. Also, in nearly all accounts William was said to have fled by means of the Underground Railroad.

That conjecture was altogether plausible, for it is recorded that runaways from areas near Martin County had in fact used that route of escape. William Still, the manager of the Philadelphia terminus of the Underground Railroad, reported that four of the nine "passengers" who arrived on July 19, 1856, were from North Carolina; and one of them, who came from Plymouth (about thirty miles from the Robeson plantations), had "left a brother in Martin county."[9]

However, it appears more likely that William's escape was made under different circumstances and that his getaway occurred not in 1860 but in 1862, during the Civil War.

North Carolina was the last of the Southern states to secede from the Union, but had it been up to the cotton and tobacco planters of Martin County that state would have jumped the gun on all the rest. On October 14, 1860, when it appeared certain that Abraham Lincoln would be elected president, the Robasons and other leading men of Martin, Edgecombe, Bertie, and Halifax Counties convened in the town of Palmyra and unanimously adopted a resolution urging immediate secession because the people of the North were "forcing . . . so-called personal liberty bills, abrogating in its entirety the fugitive slave law [and] threatening the most sacred institutions of the Southern States." Committees were named for each district to prepare for the eagerly awaited hostilities, and in the Robasons' district two of the five committeemen were Henry B. and Henry D. Robason.[10]

No doubt the two Henrys and the other slaveholding Robasons and their fellows were overjoyed seven months later (May 20, 1861) when North Carolina joined the Confederacy and entered the war, but their joy did not last the summer. On August 28 of that year there came tidings that filled the Big House with fearful dismay and the slave cabins with hopeful joy. For the first time in their lives Benjamin and Sabra and William and his brothers and sisters and the thousands of other black slaves in Martin County had something this side of Heaven to shout Glory Hallelujah about—the Yankees had captured Fort Hatteras, gateway to the coastal waters of North Carolina. Here surely was cause to sing with ecstatic (though necessarily restrained) fervor their old-time song of hoped-for liberation:

> Oh, Mary, don't yo' weep, don't yo' moan,
> Oh, Mary, don't yo' weep, don't yo' moan,
> Pharaoh's army got drownded,
> Oh, Mary, don't you' weep!

A similar fervor, though heartily unrestrained, was shown by fourteen former slaves from Virginia who manned a deck gun on the *U.S.S. Minnesota,* flagship of the victorious Union naval task force, of whom it was said, "no gun in the fleet was more steady than theirs."[11] Among the rebel troops who surrendered in this, their first, engagement were 161 volunteers from Martin County, including six Robasons and one Roberson, all of whom were privates and hence presumably not slaveowners.*[12]

---

* A North Carolina slaveowner doubtless expressed the views of his class when, explaining why he was not in uniform, he wrote: "[Since] I can't stand it as a 'private' and I see no chance of being either Capt or Lieut Grimes I am afraid I am doomed to weigh

Within a few months after the fall of Fort Hatteras the Union forces had captured several coastal ports, and thousands of slaves began to run away from their masters to seek freedom under the Stars and Stripes at the towns of Plymouth, New Bern, and other federal beachheads. In August 1862, one year after the debacle on Cape Hatteras, it was estimated by a Confederate general that slaves whose aggregate value was at least $1 million were running away to the Union Army bases in North Carolina.[13] Taking into account the depreciated market value of slaves in that state following Lincoln's election (prices fell 40 to 50 percent), it can be reckoned that William Robeson represented about $738 of that loss. (That estimate is based upon the prices at a contemporary auction near Raleigh, where an eighteen-year-old male slave was sold for $755, and another, who was fifteen, brought $705.[14] William was seventeen when he ran away and reduced his property value to zero.)

The financial loss suffered by the owners of human property in Martin County was calamitous. According to a descendant of the slaveholding Robasons, "Just about all the niggers from around here ran off to the Yankees at Plymouth."[15] Another goal for the fugitives was New Bern, a port at the mouth of the Neuse River, about sixty miles from the Robason plantations. That city was captured by the Union Army in March 1862, and within three months some 7,500 runaways had arrived there.[16]

Among the fugitives who thronged to New Bern from Martin County was Ezekiel Roberson,* who was an older brother of William Robeson. Ezekiel, who lived until the 1920s, told his grandson, Vernon Roberson, that when the Yankee army took New Bern he was one of those who took off to join them there.[17] It seems probable, then, that the escaping Ezekiel was accompanied by William; and indeed the name "William Roberson" was listed on several rosters of ex-slaves in New Bern.

"William Roberson"—in all likelihood the William Robeson of this account—was one of the hundreds of black fugitives who were hired by the Union Army to build fortifications and to work as woodcutters, teamsters, longshoremen, cooks, and laundresses.[18] Free in fact if not yet in law, the runaways, who were termed "contrabands" (i.e., enemy property sub-

---

cotton & whip negroes when shooting the damned abolitionists would be much more pleasant pastime." Quoted in James H. Boykin, *North Carolina in 1861* (New York: Bookman Associates, 1961), p. 46.

* That spelling of the surname was retained by Ezekiel Roberson and his descendants, whereas his brothers William, Benjamin, and John and their descendants dropped the second "r."

ject to seizure), were paid $10 a month. The pay was the same as that given to black troops in the Union Army (whites got $13), but to William and his fellows there was something infinitely more important than the amount of their wages. For the first time in their lives they were getting paid for their work. Thus, several years before the enactment of the Thirteenth Amendment, the abolition of unpaid slave labor was set forth not in the exalted language of constitutional law but in the dollars-and-cents accounts of "Persons and Articles Hired" by the U.S. Army.

On the payroll of Captain William Holden, quartermaster at New Bern, William was listed in a crew of runaways that included carpenters, loggers, and teamsters. Probably William was a teamster, for in later life he would show a proficiency in handling horses. There is some reason to believe that the young man may also have been one of a number whose work took them deep into Confederate-held territory. "Upwards of fifty volunteers of the best and most courageous," the superintendent of the contrabands reported, "were kept constantly employed on the perilous but important duty of spies, scouts and guides."[19] (Paul Robeson once recalled his father telling him that on two occasions during slavery-time he had returned to the Robason plantation to visit his mother, Sabra. Those visits may have been during scouting missions.)

Another activity of the runaways at New Bern may have given rise to the assertion, expressed in various writings about Paul Robeson, that his father had enlisted in the Union Army after fleeing from bondage. No evidence to support that story has been found.[20] However, William may have been one of the many black men at New Bern who on various occasions volunteered to serve as armed defenders of the base against enemy assaults. A notable example of that service was cited by Major General Oliver O. Howard of the Union Army:

> In February, 1864, while there were about two thousand freed people in the villages outside of the New Bern, N.C., intrenchments, an enterprising Confederate general, George E. Pickett, with a division of troops, attempted to retake that city. . . . Negroes, to the number of nine hundred, were put into the trenches with the white soldiers, and were highly complimented for their uniformly brave conduct during the assault. The attempt of General Pickett failed, and the negro defenders received a due proportion of credit for the repulse.*[21]

---

* Among a number of defenders captured by the repulsed Confederates were fourteen blacks. Their fate is unreported, but that it probably was a cruel one is suggested by the

(That "enterprising Confederate general" had won dubious glory the previous summer at the battle of Gettysburg, where three-fourths of his division of Virginians were mowed down in the famous—and incredibly stupid—charge associated with his name.)

Many black women were among the fugitives at New Bern, and one of these was William's sister, Margaret, who like their father, Benjamin, used the surname "Congleton." We have no knowledge as to her age or whether she accompanied one or both of her brothers in escaping from their owners in Martin County, but in view of the close familial feeling that existed among the black Robesons, a joint departure might be presumed. All that is known of her in New Bern is a single payroll entry showing that Margaret Congleton was paid $10 for the month of January 1865 as one of several women cooks in the Army's camps for the contrabands.[22] (Years later, around the turn of the century, Rev. William Robeson took his only daughter, Marian Marguerite, on a trip from their home in Princeton, New Jersey, to Martin County to visit that sister for whom he had given Marian her middle name; and Marian recalled seeing a field of cotton for the first time and having her Aunt Margaret show her how cotton was picked.)

One consequence of the Civil War was that in the Federal Census of 1870 the vast majority of African Americans who had been slaves were for the first time counted as persons with names. That census in Martin County showed William's father, Benjamin, age 50, as a farmhand, living with his wife, Sabra, 45, and three minor children, who were also listed as farmhands—Hannah, 16; Easter (erroneously spelled "Esther"), 14; and John, 12. Counted as a separate family living in the household were Ezekiel (William's brother, who had returned from New Bern to his birthplace, as did most of the runaways after the war), age 30, with his wife, Gatsy, and two infant children. No member of either family could read or write.[23] Ten years later the census-taker found Benjamin and Sabra with only son John still with them; and it was noted that John, whose age was given as 19, now could read and write.[24]

(When Sabra died some time later in the 1880s, her son, Rev. William D. Robeson, would inscribe a stained-glass window in his church at Princeton that still gives testimony of the slave-born son's devotion to his

---

fact that twenty-two white North Carolinians found among the Union Army prisoners were summarily hanged. See John G. Barrett, *The Civil War in North Carolina* (Chapel Hill: University of North Carolina Press, 1963), pp. 207–208.

mother. The inscription in the Witherspoon Street Presbyterian Church window reads: "IN LOVING REMEMBRANCE OF SABRA ROBESON.")

William's father married again, and the last record we have of him was the issuance in Martin County on May 31, 1889, of a marriage license to Benjamin Congleton, age 69, and Adline Gorham, 45.[25]

As for William Robeson, his name too was recorded for the first time in the 1870 census, though the enumerator misspelled his surname as "Robertson" while correctly noting that William was twenty-five, male, black, and born in North Carolina.[26] By that time, however, William had put an even greater distance between himself and the cotton fields of Martin County. He was now up North, and that he could read and write was manifest by the fact that his name was listed along with the names of the entire student body of Lincoln University in Pennsylvania.

It is not known when young William left the South. We can first place him in Pennsylvania in 1867, and the last reference to him in North Carolina was in June 1863 when his name last appeared on the New Bern quartermaster's payroll. A clue to his subsequent activity might be the fact that one month after that date, the first day schools for blacks were established behind the Union Army's lines in that area.[27] Within a year those schools would have some 3,000 students in attendance, and, from what is known about William in later life, when no sacrifice would be too great for the education of his children, there is good reason to believe that he would have jumped at the chance to be one of those eager learners.

The scant records of the period preserved at Lincoln University show that William enrolled in the school's one-year preparatory class in the fall of 1867.[28] His residence, given as nearby Chester Valley, was probably the place where, as he would tell his children, he worked as a farmhand after coming North and during summer vacations while working his way through college.[29]

In that preparatory class there were seventeen black students from cities in both the North and South, including two from California; but only eight of them would qualify for college entrance the following year, and only William Robeson and two others would successfully complete the four-year course for a bachelor of arts degree.*

---

* One of the three was William H. Bell, of Washington, D.C., who two years earlier had helped frustrate an attempt on the life of William H. Seward, secretary of state in President Lincoln's Cabinet, which had occurred simultaneously with the fatal shooting of the president on April 14, 1865. When he graduated with William Robeson's class of 1873, it was recalled that Bell "was one of Secretary Seward's attendants at the time of the

The curriculum at Lincoln, like that of the principal American colleges at the time, was modeled on the classical pattern of Oxford and Cambridge in England; and no lowering of standards was made for the all-black student body who entered the ivied halls only a few years after leaving slave-quarter cabins. For each of the four years one attended Lincoln, Latin and Greek were the twin poles of the ladder of learning that had to be climbed; and each year the climb became steeper.

William's freshman year in 1868 may have been too difficult for him, or he may not have had the means to remain in school, but whatever happened, the following year he was again listed as a freshman. Thereafter, he continued with that class. As a sophomore in 1870, when all members of his family in Martin County were recorded as being unable to read or write because of the total denial of schooling to them, William was coping with the following subjects: History; Greek Reader; Sallus (*Conspiracy of Cataline*); Geometry; Playfair's *Euclid*; Physical Geography; Xenophon (*Anabasis*); Virgil (*Aeneid*); Natural Philosophy; Rhetoric, Day's; Latin Prose Composition; and Lectures on Botany.[30]

That he mastered those studies and others that were later required (among them chemistry, astronomy, geology, trigonometry, mineralogy, political economy, and English literature) was shown when William was named one of the seven honor graduates of the Class of 1873.[31] He was also selected to be one of the speakers at the commencement exercises on June 18, 1873. But whatever he said in his belles lettres oration was as lost to history as the oration delivered in Latin by classmate Abraham P. Denny (who would be a lifelong friend of William's), of which a newspaper reporter noted: "Very few understood anything he said." The reporter, who was pleased that the classical oration of another honor student had made a strong plea for study of the classics, commented: "While so many white youth decry Latin and Greek, it is quite refreshing to hear a colored youth advocate their study. We think Harvard is setting a bad precedent in placing the classics on the list of elective studies after the freshman year. . . . The result is that after the first year in College, Latin and Greek become *non-elect* by the great majority of the students."[32]

William Robeson's own advocacy of classical studies would later be a major influence on the education of his son Paul, who recalled that his

---

attempted assassination of that gentleman in Washington, and resisted [the assailant's] entrance to Seward's house." From the *Local Daily News*, West Chester, Pa., July 2, 1873 (at Chester County Historical Society).

father "firmly believed that the heights of knowledge must be scaled by the freedom-seeker" and that "Latin, Greek, philosophy, history, literature—all the treasures of learning must be the Negro's heritage as well."[33] It is also certain that his father was an important factor in Paul's lifelong passion for the study of languages.

When after graduation William continued his studies at Lincoln's divinity school, another ancient language was a required subject in each year of the three-year course. The subject, Hebrew and Old Testament Literature, involved learning not only the grammar and syntax of that language but "the students will be exercised in the pronunciation of the Hebrew text and in exact and idiomatic translations from the Hebrew into English."[34] There is, of course, no way of knowing how proficient William Robeson became in pronouncing Old Testament Hebrew or the Hellenistic Greek of the New Testament, but it might be assumed that his success in these courses was related to the extraordinary facility later achieved by Paul Robeson in mastering the spoken word of many languages.

Along his studious way through divinity school, an extracurricular subject must at times have distracted William from the required profundities of Apologetics, Homiletics, Theology, Ecclesiastic History, Sacred Geography and Antiquities, and so on. That subject was Maria Louisa Bustill, a strikingly attractive young schoolteacher from Philadelphia who often came to Lincoln University to visit her uncle, Joseph Bustill, who kept a boardinghouse in the town and did not—as a jury once decided—sell whisky or overly strong cider to the students. ("A colored divine, a student at the college, said he had drank [Bustill's] cider, and that it had affected him in a strange manner. . . . "[35]) The divinity student in that case was not William, who, not strangely, had been deeply affected by Bustill's niece, and no doubt he became a frequent front-parlor caller at the commodious Bustill home whenever Maria Louisa was in town.

"To everything there is a season," the Old Testament advises, including "a time to embrace." But the fifth verse of Ecclesiastes 3 quickly adds that there is also "a time to refrain from embracing," and so the smitten William went on to complete his studies at Lincoln's theological department and to be awarded on June 6, 1876, the additional degrees of Master of Arts and Bachelor of Sacred Theology.[36] Having recently adopted the middle name "Drew" (perhaps from the noted actor John Drew), the former officially nameless six-year-old black male slave, who was now thirty-one, emerged from Lincoln University as the Reverend William D. Robeson, A.B., M.A., S.T.B.

Two years later, William, son of Benjamin and Sabra of Martin County, North Carolina, and Maria Louisa, daughter of Charles, granddaughter of David, and great-granddaughter of Cyrus Bustill of New Jersey and Pennsylvania, were married. Their wedding, on July 11, 1878, took place in the First African Presbyterian Church, an outgrowth of the Free African Society of which Cyrus Bustill had been a cofounder in 1787. And like their parents, William and Maria Louisa would remain together until death did them part.

৶ 3 ৶

Princeton:
The South Up North

*W*AR WAS IN THE AIR when Paul Robeson drew his first breath of
life in the parsonage of the Witherspoon Street Presbyterian Church in
Princeton, New Jersey. On that day—Saturday, April 9, 1898—the pages
of the weekly newspaper of that quiet little college town reverberated with
the thunder of the approaching storm. In three editorials the *Princeton
Press* expounded on the imminence, rightness, and seasonableness of war
with Spain.[1] "If the opening week shall see the declaration of war," the
first editorial observed, "the United States would undertake the task with
the feeling that she has never entered upon a more righteous strife." The
second editorial, after noting that the impending conflict would be waged
for the "relief of suffering Cuba" and to take a "stand for humanity," concluded: "Men might call it war, but it is in fact a struggle for peace." In
the third, entitled "The Fatal Month," the editor recalled that earlier
wars—the American Revolution, Mexican War, and Civil War—had all
begun in April, and he deemed it likely that the present April would be
added to that list. (He was right. Congress declared war on April 25.)

A brief item in the "University News" column on the next page—"Professor Woodrow Wilson delivered a lecture in Orange Music Hall, Thurs-
day evening, under the auspices of the Women's Club of Orange"—was
an omen of still another fatal April that would come nineteen years later
when that professor, having risen to become successively president of
Princeton, governor of New Jersey, and president of the United States,
would lead the nation into the even more righteous strife he termed the
"war to end all wars." And elsewhere on that page, under the bold-type

19

headline "WAR! WAR! WAR!" a resolute citizen proclaimed his stand: "Let there be war. I will stay in the Insurance Business just the same. D. Foster Updike, 82 Nassau St."

But if the editor and the businessman looked forward to government action abroad, the black community of Princeton and others throughout the land were calling upon the government to take a "stand for humanity" at home. For African Americans the so-called Gay Nineties were grim and terrible years of renewed oppression by the forces of White Supremacy that were arrayed both in the white robes of the Ku Klux Klan and the black robes of Justice. Lynch law took more African American lives in that decade than at any other time, and in 1893 the law of the Supreme Court wiped out the Civil Rights Act of 1875. Then in 1896, two years before Paul Robeson was born, the Supreme Court upheld state and local laws that compelled the separation of the races in all public facilities.*

A sign of the times that was also remarkably prophetic of a notable incident in Paul Robeson's life was a news story that appeared on the day of his birth in one of the black weeklies. On April 9, 1898, the *Cleveland Gazette* reported that a delegation had gone to the White House to demand that President William McKinley take action to stop the wave of lynchings in the South and that the black spokeswoman, Ida B. Wells, who had "agitated the subject of lynching both in this country and Great Britain," told the president:

> Nowhere in the civilized world save the United States of America do men, possessing all civil and political power, go out in bands of 50 to 5,000 to hunt down, shoot, hang or burn to death a single individual, unarmed and absolutely powerless. Statistics show that nearly 10,000 American citizens have been lynched in the past 20 years. . . . We refuse to believe that this country, so powerful to defend its citizens abroad, is unable to protect its citizens at home.[2]

(Fifty years later, after he himself had "agitated the subject of lynching both in this country and Great Britain"—and around the world—Robeson would stand before another president in the White House and, as a

---

* The blatant racism of the Supreme Court in *Plessy v. Ferguson* was denounced in the dissenting opinion of Justice John M. Harlan, who wrote: "What can more certainly arouse hate . . . and perpetuate a feeling of distrust between these races, than State enactments, which, in fact, proceed upon the grounds that colored citizens are so inferior that they cannot be allowed to sit in public coaches occupied by white citizens?"

militant spokesman for black Americans, demand action on that same grievance.)

However, on that day in Princeton the assured promise of glorious war abroad and the broken promise of freedom at home were alike forgotten at the parsonage at 72 Witherspoon Street,* where the Reverend William D. Robeson, who was nearly fifty-three, and his wife, Maria Louisa, forty-five, rejoiced in the birth of their seventh and last child, whom they would name Paul Leroy.

The Robesons' first child, Gertrude Lascet, had been born in the parsonage nineteen years earlier, only a month after Rev. Robeson brought his wife to Princeton in September 1879 and became pastor of the Presbyterian church in the black community. But Gertrude died in infancy, as did their third child, Peter Charles, who was born in 1884. Of the surviving children, William D. Robeson Jr., the second-born and oldest when Paul was born, was going on seventeen. John Bunyan Reeve, who hated that resounding name and insisted on being called simply "Reeve," was twelve; Benjamin Congleton was in his sixth year, and the only girl, Marian Marguerite, was going on four.

Residing nearby were two more Robeson families, headed by brothers of William who had followed him to Princeton from North Carolina. Next door to the parsonage, at 71 Witherspoon Street, were Benjamin Robeson; his wife, Huldah; and their children; and around the corner, within the same block at 22 Green Street, were John Robeson; his wife, Hattie; and their children.[3] Like most of the town's black residents, Paul Robeson's Uncle Ben and Uncle John were listed in the city directory as laborers.

At the time Paul was born, his brother Ben and his sister, Marian, were still too young for school, but his brother Reeve and four Robeson cousins (one of them a girl named Sabra) were enrolled in the segregated Witherspoon Street Public School.[4] Paul's oldest brother, Bill (William D., Jr.), was attending high school, but because black students were barred from the secondary school in Princeton, Bill had to travel each day to Trenton, eleven miles away, to get the education Rev. Robeson sought for his children. Thus when Paul was a year old there came a memorable day for his parents, uncles, aunts, and cousins and for the black community as a whole: On June 27, 1899, Bill became the first youth from their commu-

---

* Redesignated later as No. 110, Paul Robeson's birthplace still stands at the corner of Witherspoon and Green Streets.

nity to graduate from high school.[5] White Princeton also noted the occasion, its newspaper reporting with civic pride and no hint of civic shame the news that William D. Robeson Jr. of Princeton graduated with high honors from the high school of Trenton.[6]

It was not law but tradition that made Princeton a Jim Crow town. From its earliest days the town had a relatively large number of black residents, and in an article on that subject that appeared during Paul Robeson's childhood, the *Princeton Press,* after noting that blacks comprised nearly a fifth of the town's 4,000 official residents, went on to say: "A writer to *Harper's Monthly* in the [eighteen-] fifties jocularly said that if in passing through New Jersey a traveler came to a place where there were two darkies to every white man and two dogs to every negro, he might be sure he was in Princeton."[7]

Had that wayfarer also felt sure that he had come to a place in the Deep South, he would have been only technically wrong. Princeton University was essentially a Southern institution, for it drew its well-to-do student body largely from below the Mason-Dixon line. Princeton—college and town—was like the Big House of a Southern plantation, with the black townspeople as its servants, and consequently the close-but-distant relationship of master and man was the general pattern.

Paternalism and Calvinism combined to enroll blacks as members of the First Presbyterian Church of Princeton from its beginning in 1766, though racism relegated them to balcony seats that were both closer to Heaven and farther from the preacher and the white congregation. But seventy years later, when the old church burned down and a new one was erected, it was deemed that even the balcony was not far enough away. Dr. James W. Alexander, a Princeton professor and a notable figure in the history of the town and church, explained the change in a letter to a friend in 1837:

> We have a new and handsome edifice. While it was building the negroes worshipped apart, in a little place of their own. The majority of the pew-holders wish them to remain a separate congregation. . . . If they come back, they will take up about half the gallery. There are about 80 black communicants. I am clear that in a church of Jesus Christ there is neither black nor white; and that we have no right to consider the accident of colour in any degree. Yet I think the blacks very unwise in insisting on such a privilege now. Some years ago there would not have been the slightest difficulty in admitting them, but in consequence of the abolition movements the prejudice of the lower classes of whites against the blacks has become exorbitant and inhuman.[8]

Unwisely or not, the black members stubbornly resisted their exclusion for several years but finally yielded to the inevitable, and in 1846 the First Presbyterian Church of Color was set up for them. Two years later its congregation changed the name to Witherspoon Street Presbyterian Church and raised the money to reimburse the white philanthropists who had paid for the construction of the separate house of worship. One of the black trustees, described as a "civil, intelligent and honest man [who had] kept an ice cream saloon, oyster cellar and confectionery on Nassau Street," bequeathed to the church a house—one of six he had acquired—for use as a parsonage.[9] Located on the other end of the block from that parsonage, where Paul Robeson was born, was the church that his father served as pastor for twenty-one years. The church, which still stands at the corner of Witherspoon and Quarry Streets, is a small wooden structure, painted white, with the traditional steeple and stained-glass windows that are not arched but squared at the top in the simple design of early American churches.

"That church carved out of ebony," as the local newspaper once referred to it,[10] was the principal center for the black community in which Rev. Robeson became the leading figure. In later years black Baptist and Methodist churches were established by newcomers from the South, but because Princeton was Presbyterian, Rev. Robeson's church had the greatest influence with the upper-class whites who dominated the town.

Then too in that college town Rev. Robeson's erudition had to command a certain respect. For example, two years after the minister had begun his pastorate, the *Princeton Press* published a lengthy excerpt from his sermon on the assassination of President James Garfield along with sermons on that subject delivered by the town's leading white ministers. In his discourse, described as "breathing the purest patriotism, just, timely and kind in sentiment, all well expressed," Rev. Robeson used the occasion to speak out against lynchings. "There are men and women," he said, "who, when they speak of the assassin [a disgruntled office-seeker], wax warm with wrath and indignation and speak strongly of taking the law into their own hands. Let no such act as mob violence or lynch law blot anew the escutcheon of our noble land."[11]

The second most prestigious post in the black community—principal of the black public school—was held by one of Rev. Robeson's Lincoln University classmates, Abraham P. Denny (whose commencement-day Latin oration was reportedly little understood by the audience). Denny, who had arrived in Princeton not long after Rev. Robeson, became an elder in his classmate's church and served for nineteen years as head of the school.

By all accounts the two leaders served the black community well during the two decades of their service, and though they retained the strong backing of their people, the time came when Robeson and Denny lost the goodwill of those from whom all earthly blessings flowed. Then, as if they were household servants deemed to have become too uppity in their ways, the black preacher and principal were summarily dismissed from their positions. No doubt the local white power structure was greatly offended by the leading roles both men played on one occasion when, as the *Princeton Press* reported, "The colored people of Princeton assembled in mass meeting in the Witherspoon St. Presbyterian Church on Tuesday evening last [November 29, 1898] to discuss the recent violent race disturbances in several of our States, especially in the States of North Carolina and South Carolina."[12] (In addition to sharing the general community sentiment on that subject, William Robeson had an urgent personal concern: His brother, Ezekiel, his sister, Margaret, and many others of his kin were still "down home" in Martin County, North Carolina, where their lives were endangered by the widespread antiblack terror.)

Rev. Robeson and the pastors of the black Baptist and the African Methodist Episcopal (A.M.E.) churches were the speakers at that rally, and according to the newspaper story their

> addresses were carefully prepared and eloquently delivered. . . . They advocated no violence, no retaliation, they opposed violence in every form. They thought there should be Christian sentiment enough to prevent such disgraceful outrages. They thought it possible to enact laws to enable the general government to protect all its citizens.
>
> The Secretary [school principal Denny] read a series of resolutions protesting against the outrages, deploring mob violence, appealing to the President to use all the power he possesses in the interest of law and order, [and] to Congress to enact necessary laws. . . . After the adoption of the resolution the speakers above mentioned [the Reverends W. D. Robeson, S. W. Smith, and R. W. Fickland] were named as delegates to attend a mass meeting in Philadelphia on Thursday, December 1st, for the same purpose as was this one.

On that evening, a block away at the parsonage, a seven-month-old future protester against lynch law was probably fast asleep in his crib; or, if he had already developed his lifelong habit of staying up late, Paul Robeson may have been babbling away in musical baby talk. By the militant standard of this son's later speeches, Rev. Robeson's remarks at that rally were no doubt exceedingly mild. But in that time and place—the

Princeton that earlier had banished from its church balcony seats the black members because of the rise of the subversive "abolition movements" (as mentioned in the cited letter of Dr. Alexander) and had barred black students from both high school and college—the nonviolent remarks of Rev. Robeson and the resolutions introduced by Abraham Denny must have seemed as intolerably radical to the town's ruling whites as any black protest would have seemed in the Bourbon South.

Eighteen months later the ax came down on the school principal. Noting that "Mr. Denny's character is above reproach, and he has been well liked by the colored people,"* the *Press* reported that the board of education had appointed a new principal for the Witherspoon Street School.[13] The paper was certain that the all-white board "was solely actuated by a desire to do [the] best for the pupils," but its account indicated that the black citizens had a strongly differing opinion that was expressed at a mass meeting held at the A.M.E. church "to protest against the action of the Board in . . . getting rid of Prof. Denny." A committee of community leaders headed by Rev. Robeson was delegated to go to the board meeting the following week to ask that the ouster be rescinded. That was in June 1900, and evidently the rejection of a petition from the powerless black community was too commonplace to be newsworthy, because the next—and last—item about the matter did not appear until October: "Mr. A. P. Denny, former principal," was leaving town, and his departure "will be a sad one to his many friends in Princeton."[14]

The saddest of all must have been William Robeson. Not only was he losing his longtime friend and coworker but he must have known that his own ouster was near at hand. After two decades of dedicated service to his congregation and community he was to be struck down by the men in power. How could he face the impending blow to the profound pride and dignity he had gained in his heroic climb from slavery to distinction? Then too there was his family situation. By straining every resource, he now had his son Bill in college (he would graduate in 1902). On his meager salary[†] Rev. Robeson also had to support four minor children at home and his afflicted wife. (Maria Louisa, who had taught at the public school

---

* It might be noted that Princeton's newspaper, unlike any in the actual South, accorded blacks the designation of "Mr."

† The Witherspoon Street Presbyterian Church has no records of Rev. Robeson's many years of service there, but his low salary is indicated by the fact that a succeeding pastor's salary was raised $5 a month to provide an annual pay of $700 (*Princeton Press*, June 30, 1906).

when the couple first came to Princeton, was now a near invalid, suffering from asthma and growing blind as a result of cataracts.)

The blow came less than a month after Denny's departure. On November 8, 1900, a proposal to oust Rev. Robeson was brought to his congregation at a meeting that "was entirely under the charge of the Rev. Dr. Wm. Brenton Greene," a member of the all-white governing body of the local Presbyterians.[15] (A faction within the church—its size is unknown—was willing to accede to the ouster, but for the most part, perhaps out of shame, the members of that group were not present.) After reporting that those in attendance had voted with near unanimity in favor of retaining their pastor (only two persons were opposed), the news account of the meeting concluded: "Dr. Greene will report the result to the Presbytery at their next meeting . . . November 12, when decisive action will be taken."

The decisive action of the Big House was swift in coming. Five days after the Presbytery met, the *Press* told the whole story in the two sentences it published: "The Rev. Wm. D. Robeson has resigned the pastorate of the Witherspoon Street Presbyterian Church, to take effect on February 1. The church will continue the salary and the use of the parsonage, if needed, until May 1."[16]

The end of the nineteenth century thus marked the end of William Robeson's leadership in Princeton. The incoming century would soon find him knocked down into the dust—literally so, as we shall see. In the first month of that new era, on January 27, 1901, every seat in the pews and gallery of his church was occupied, chairs and benches were placed in the aisles, and many people had to stand in the rear when Rev. Robeson preached his farewell sermon. In his remarks, to which the *Press* gave a generous amount of space,* the deposed pastor, who felt "this evening as one about to say the last words to friends before taking a long journey," made no mention of the Presbytery's action. After expressing his sorrow that some members of his church "in the hours of its darkest need forsook it," he reviewed his twenty-one-year pastorate and thanked all who had worked with him as well as those who had come from the other black congregations to stand with him on this occasion. In concluding, he enjoined his hearers—as he must have been telling his own heavy heart—"Do not be discouraged, do not think your past work is in vain. . . . Gird

---

* It would seem to be the kind of generosity Fyodor Dostoyevsky had in mind when he wrote: "Men reject their prophets and slay them, but they love their martyrs and honor those they have slain."

on your armor and with renewed courage strive to do well the work the Master has assigned to you, daring ever to do right, to be true; remembering you each have a work to do that no other can do, and doing it so kindly, so truly, so well, angels will hasten the story to tell."[17] (The spirit of that injunction would be invoked a half-century later by William Robeson's youngest son, Paul, after he, too, in effect had been deposed. "My Pop's influence is still present in the struggles of today," Paul Robeson wrote in 1952. "I know he would say, 'Stand firm, son; stand by your principles.'" Then Paul added: "You bet I will, Pop—as long as there is a breath in my body."[18])

The solidarity of the community was demonstrated at that assemblage by the participation of the pastors of the Bright Hope Baptist Church and the Mount Pisgah A.M.E. Church. As he listened to their words of sympathy and support Rev. Robeson must have reflected on the fact that although those leaders, like all in the black community, were governed by the white Establishment, as pastors of independent black churches they could not be so readily forced from their pulpits as he had been.

Two weeks later one final grace was granted by the local newspaper when it published the text of a lengthy statement in praise of Rev. Robeson by his former congregation. Asserting that "by his precepts and example many were led to pure and honorable lives," the tribute gratefully noted his work in the community "to relieve the wretched, the poor, the sick, the unfortunate, rather than pile up riches for himself." The statement concluded: "As a church session we deeply regret his severance from us [and] trust that in the providence of God there is a large field awaiting his services."[19]

However, for the poor black people of Princeton the providence of God was narrowly limited by the social structure. The providence of man (or rather The Man, as the folk expression termed the power structure) decreed that the only large field awaiting the services of the Reverend Mr. William Drew Robeson, A.B., M.A., S.T.B., in that town was the field of menial labor. So when he changed his family's residence from the parsonage to a house around the corner on Green Street he also changed his garb from the traditional black frock coat of the minister to the blue denim overalls worn by laborers like his brothers, Ben and John. Rev. Robeson—the title would remain as much a part of him as his patriarchal manner—was now in his fifty-sixth year. Fortunately for his wife and children, his strength of body (he was broad of shoulders and powerfully built) was equal to his strength of spirit when, like evicted Adam, he was in effect commanded: *In the sweat of thy face shalt thou eat bread.*

Along with that lesson from Genesis, Rev. Robeson may have remembered that Virgil had bravely counseled *Labor omnia vincit* (Labor conquers all). But more likely on his mind at that time was the bleak realism of Homer that he had translated from the Greek in his third year at Lincoln: "Toil is the lot of all, and bitter woe/The fate of many." (This said essentially the same thing as the African American saying that William and his unschooled brothers had learned as childhood field hands: "Life is short and full of blisters.") At any rate, Rev. Robeson bought a horse and wagon and began to earn a living hauling ashes from the homes of the townspeople.

Paul Leroy Robeson* was then three years old, too young to know anything about his father's tragic downfall. The first occupation he saw his father engaged in was that of ashman: "This was his work at the time I first remember him and I recall the growing mound of dusty ashes dumped into our back yard at 13 Green Street. A fond memory remains of our horse, a mare named Bess, whom I grew to love and who loved me. My father also went into the hack business, and as a coachman drove the gay young students around town and on trips to the seashore."[20] And the son remembered: "Not once did I hear him complain of the poverty and misfortune of those years. Not one word of bitterness ever came from him."

When Paul was nearly six an even more grievous blow was suffered by the stoical William Robeson and his family. On January 19, 1904, Maria Louisa Robeson was fatally burned in a household accident. Rev. Robeson was away for the day, on a shopping trip to Trenton; and though it was a school day, his son Ben, who was eleven, had stayed at home to help his nearly blind mother. The two oldest sons—Bill, who was twenty-two, and Reeve, eighteen—were away at college (Bill at the University of Pennsylvania Medical School and Reeve at Lincoln, of which both his father and Bill were alumni); and the girl, Marian, who was nine, was in class at the nearby Witherspoon Street Public School. Also in school that day was Marian's ten-year-old cousin, Virgie. Years later that cousin, Mrs.

---

* Paul Robeson would use his middle name through college and drop it when he became an actor. Then he would admit to the "Leroy" only when it was necessary to refute the frequent mistaken listing of his middle name as "Bustill"—an error that keenly distressed him. The principal source of the error, which appeared in *Current Biography* and other reference publications, was his wife's giving his name as Paul "Bustill" Robeson in her biography of him. Eslanda Robeson evidently preferred the family name of the proud Bustills to the commonplace middle name Paul had when they were married.

Virginia Bustill Smith Rhetta, recalled in vivid detail what happened that
wintry day in Princeton.[21]

Aunt Lou, as Virgie called her mother's cousin, had asked young Ben
to help her put a piece of new linoleum under the coal-burning parlor
stove, and when the door of the tipped stove flew open some hot coals
ignited Mrs. Robeson's dress. In an instant she was engulfed in flames.
The terrified Ben tried to beat out the blaze and then ran into the street
screaming for help. Neighbors rushed into the house, and someone ran
out and got a bucket of snow to spill on the badly burned victim. Together
with Marian, Virgie ran to the house when news of the accident reached
them at school.

"I can never forget," Virginia Rhetta said after the passage of more
than three-score years, "the smell of burned flesh that filled the house
when we ran in." Virgie's mother, Anna Bustill Smith (the principal
Bustill family historian), had rushed to her cousin's aid and had folded
back into place some of the charred flesh that had fallen away from the
injured woman's thigh. "Aunt Lou knew she was dying, but she told
Mama that she wanted to stay alive until Reverend Robeson got home
so that she could talk with him about plans for their children. Well, she
did see him and then afterward the doctor gave her medicine to kill the
pain and she lost consciousness and died at four o'clock in the morning."

Strangely, no one—not Virginia Rhetta or Marian Robeson or anyone
else—remembered where Paul was on that day of searing pain for the living and the dying. He himself had no memory of his mother, and if, as
was likely, he was at home amid the screams and the smoke and the people rushing in and out, the traumatic events must have caused him to
blot it all out of his mind forever. Once, long after, a woman came up to
him after he had sung at the Harlem church where his brother Ben (the
Reverend B. C. Robeson) was pastor, and said: "You don't know me. I'm
your cousin from North Carolina. I remember you as a baby, when your
mother came down to visit us. Do you remember?" When Paul told of
that encounter, he mused: "Do I remember? Yes, rather hazily—[there
were] Aunt Margaret, Uncle Zeke [his father's older brother, Ezekiel],
and tens and tens of my relatives living on the very soil where my father
had been a slave."[22] But of his mother he had not even a hazy recollection.

The widower William Robeson was now fifty-nine, and it might be
expected that he would have no other ambition in life beyond seeing that
each of his children got an education and the opportunity to fulfill whatever potentialities they might have. Underlying the concept of being true

to one's principles, which Paul learned from his father, was Rev. Robeson's insistence on personal integrity. Oddly enough, the main precept he taught Paul—and more by example than by word—came not from Scripture but from Shakespeare. "To thine own self be true"—that was the main thing: to measure oneself by one's own potential rather than by the yardstick of others.

To be true to himself, William Robeson, who had lost his position of leadership and then suffered the greater loss of his devoted wife and coworker, was determined to find that "large field awaiting his services" that his former congregation had wished for him. And while he made the dusty rounds of his daily toil, Rev. Robeson kept his self-confidence bright within his heart and was firmly resolved to rise from those ashes to a place of leadership among his people once again.

4

Happy Black Boy

𝒯HE ASHMAN'S YOUNGEST SON was a happy child. If Paul ever grieved at the loss of the mother he did not remember, he could never have felt "a long ways from home" as did the motherless child in the plaintive Negro spiritual he would sing in concerts. In Paul's case "home" was all around him in the black community where he was born, and indeed, as Paul said, if one were to list all of the people who helped raise him, "it would read like the roster of Negro Princeton."[1] In addition to all of those who called one another "brother" and "sister" as church members and treated with avuncular fondness their former pastor's little boy, Paul was surrounded by many actual relatives in the neighborhood of Green Street. And not only were there the children of Uncle Ben and Uncle John, but there were also numerous cousins surnamed Carraway and Chance whose parents had followed their Robeson relatives from Martin County to Princeton. As Paul remembered: "My early youth was spent hugged to the hearts and bosoms of my hard-working relatives. Mother died when I was six, but just across the street were my cousins the Carraways, with many children—Sam, Martha, Cecelia. And I remember the cornmeal, greens, yams, and the peanuts and other goodies sent up in bags from down in North Carolina."[2] And whenever his father's work as a coachman took him out of town (it was more than forty miles to the seaside resorts of Long Beach or Asbury Park) Paul would be left in the care of any one of a dozen different households that were like home to him.

(One of those homes was visited by Paul Robeson in 1952—almost forty years after his mother's death—when he undertook to show this writer the scenes of his childhood that he himself had not seen for many years. One of the persons on Green Street who stopped to shake his hand told him that a certain Mrs. Staton was doing poorly and asked if he would like to see her. Of course he would, he said; he was then led to a small frame house nearby wherein a very old woman lay. So frail she barely made a mound beneath the blanket, Mrs. Staton looked up at the visitor, whose massive bulk seemed to fill the tiny bedroom, and cried out: "Paul! Paul! Oh, come here, boy!" And as he bent over to kiss her, she slowly raised her arms, so thin, dry-brown, and withered, to gently embrace him. "Paul, boy," she whispered weakly, "I could crush every bone in your body!" Then as she sank back she looked at him with loving wonder and murmured, "You know, I used to hold you in my arms when you was just a little baby." Later Paul explained to me that Mrs. Staton was the sister of his Uncle Ben's wife, Huldah, and that the old lady was one of those who had cared for him as a child.)

However, at the center of everything for the boy was his father's gentle love and firm direction. After the death of his wife, Rev. Robeson sent his son Ben and daughter, Marian, to boarding schools in North Carolina, where except for vacations Ben would stay through high school and college, and Marian through high school. (Marian would later attend a training school for teachers in Pennsylvania.) Thus, with his two oldest brothers—Bill and Reeve—away at college, only Paul was always at home with his father; and under that circumstance a close bond developed between the boy and the man who was old enough to be his grandfather. Everything about the man he called "Pop" was a shining glory to Paul, whose eyes would fill with tears whenever he spoke of the man he remembered as the embodiment of human goodness. Pop's character was of "rocklike strength and dignity," and he had "the greatest speaking voice I have ever heard . . . a deep sonorous basso, richly melodic and refined."[3] Paul's lifelong habit of identifying every achievement with thoughts of his father no doubt began in childhood when he was filled with pride to walk hand in hand with Pop and to share the glow of respect and love that flashed on people's faces as they greeted the pair.

The communal love that came to Paul was also a legacy from his mother—the "Aunt Lou" of the neighborhood—who had for many years been Rev. Robeson's active partner in the various duties they assumed in the absence of other social agencies—visiting the sick and bedridden; collecting food, clothing, and fuel for the destitute; interceding with the authorities on behalf of juvenile offenders; and finding jobs for the steady stream of refugees from the land of terror in the South. Maria Louisa Robeson had, like her husband, been greatly respected for her book-learning; too, she had been a schoolteacher, an occupation that was exceeded in prestige only by the positions of pastor and school principal.

As Paul remembered it, there was something mystical and strangely prophetic in the community's attitude toward him. The people seemed to feel that there was something special about him, that he was somehow destined for big things in life. Apart from any intuitive foresight that may have been involved (and Paul would always give great weight to intuition) the people had doubtlessly come to the stock conclusion that an obedient, dutiful, and respectful child like Paul, who was being raised by a man who preached and practiced "doing right," was bound to grow up to "amount to something"—the highest level of which was to become "a credit to the race." Folk wisdom in such matters has, of course, the infallibility of "heads I win, tails you lose," because that body of knowledge encompasses many mutually contradictory ideas. Thus the black community of Princeton, which was sure the preacher's son Paul was bound for earthly glory, no doubt also firmly held to the folklore of such communities that foretold that a preacher's son was certain to go wrong. And sure enough, John Bunyan Reeve Robeson, the second oldest son in the family, did become an example to prove that rule.

When Reeve (he was nicknamed "Reed" by his family and friends) decided as a child to drop the churchly "John Bunyan" part of his name,* it may have been a foreboding to Rev. Robeson that he would have trouble in keeping that independent-minded boy on the path of righteousness. For a youngster to be righteous, public school was no less important than Sunday school in the dogma of William Robeson's generation, to whom education, like Jesus, was "the truth, the light and the way." Rising from the depths of chattel slavery and aspiring to the heights of full equality, the freedmen were strong in their belief that the enforced ignorance of enslavement was a bond to be broken along with the physical shackles. Thus to Rev. Robeson it must have been not only a keen personal disappointment but the rankest of heresies for Reeve to leave college and not graduate with the Class of 1907, with which he had started.

The circumstances of Reeve's failure are not known. If, as may happen with a preacher's son, Reeve had become surfeited with the religious environment at home, he would have found no change at college. Lincoln University, like other church-sponsored colleges for blacks, made chapel attendance compulsory, and there was little exaggeration in the complaint

---

* When William Robeson named his son after that seventeenth-century, nonconformist English preacher and author, he could never have imagined how much of a nonconformist that boy would become.

of students that chapel was three times every day and all day Sunday. Then too, if Reeve for certain lacked his father's do-or-die motivation to master the difficult curriculum, he may also have lacked the aptitude for study that characterized the other Lincoln graduate in the family—his brother Bill.

When the prodigal son came home, he probably did not dare say to his father that without a college diploma he was just as qualified for the work available to a black man in Princeton as was Rev. Robeson with all three of his degrees. That obvious truth was quickly demonstrated when, with the help of his father, Reeve got a horse and carriage and became a hack driver. But Reeve lacked the iron self-control that such a job required. A former slave like his father had had to learn early in life that to survive he must close his mind to verbal abuse by a master, but when Ol' Massa's student-sons at Princeton spoke abusively to him, Reeve would seek to teach self-control rather than to practice it. A passenger who directed some racist epithet to that driver or sought to make him the object of some joke about "darkies" could quickly find himself hauled from his seat and reprimanded by Reeve's fists. And if a group of offenders was involved, Reeve would vigorously lay about him with the bag of rocks he always carried under his seat.

Scorning the social laws of caste behavior, the rebellious Reeve became increasingly scornful of law in general, and from time to time it became the embarrassing duty of the dignified Rev. Robeson to go to court and try to get his son out of trouble. To young Paul that wayward brother, so quick with his fists to challenge any slight, was as admirable as Bill, who was always best in his classes, or Ben, the star of the neighborhood with a baseball and bat.

As a scholar and a clergyman Rev. Robeson was, of course, a man of peace. He would lead community actions against injustices, but to him individual acts of violence were both futile and immoral; and Reeve must often have heard him cite Matthew 26:52 wherein the Master counseled: "Put up again thy sword into his place: for all they that take the sword shall perish with the sword." And the Old Testament made things very clear when it advised Reeve that "A wise son *heareth* his father's instruction: but a scorner heedeth not rebuke" (Proverbs 13:1). The Bible likewise advised his father what to do about a heedless son: "Cast out the scorner, and contention shall go out" (Proverbs, 22:10).

Reeve had to be cast out. Not mainly because of the contention caused by Reeve's scofflaw ways, but because of Rev. Robeson's worry that his second-oldest son would be a bad example for his innocent youngest. At

Rev. Robeson's insistence, Reeve left town.* Paul would never forget the advice Reeve once gave him: "Don't ever take low. Stand up to them and hit back harder than they hit you." And years after the brother's death Paul would note that though Reeve "won no honors in classroom, pulpit or platform . . . I remember him with love."[4]

When Paul was eight and a pupil at the segregated public school that his brothers and sisters had attended, his father made a momentous decision: In 1906 Rev. Robeson changed his church affiliation from the Presbytery of New Brunswick, which had removed him as pastor five years earlier, to the New Jersey Conference of the African Methodist Episcopal Zion Church—an independent black denomination founded in New York in 1796.[5] The following year Rev. Robeson, at the age of sixty-two (which was far beyond the average life expectancy at the time) decided to leave Princeton, where he had lived for nearly thirty years, and build elsewhere a new church in his new denomination and begin all over again as a pastor among his people. Taking young Paul with him, the old man moved to the town of Westfield, New Jersey, which happily for his son was only about thirty miles from all his uncles, aunts, cousins, and friends in Princeton.

Westfield, though larger than Princeton, had a much smaller black population, of whom fewer than a dozen were adherents of the A.M.E. Zion denomination. Together with that little band of followers, Rev. Robeson dug the foundation for the church building that would rise when and if the money could be raised. As the bishop who assigned him to that unpromising post must have known, William Robeson was a remarkable fund-raiser. (In their farewell tribute to him, his old congregation in Princeton had noted that he was "an excellent financier" who "in many instances came to the relief of officers and congregation when the raising of needful funds seemed an impossibility."[6]) The seemingly impossible task in Westfield was also accomplished, and in 1908, a year after Rev. Robeson's arrival, the St. Luke's A.M.E. Zion Church was erected, together with a parsonage for the wonder-working pastor.†

The enormous pride and joy that must have filled the heart of the recent ashman-coachman as he rose again to a leading position did not manifest itself in any outward jubilation, and to his sensitive young son,

---

* Reeve moved to Detroit, where he is said to have gone into business. The nature of that business is not known, and when Paul met Reeve there in later years he tactfully did not ask about his brother's enterprise.

† That church still stands on Downer Street at the corner of Osborn Street.

Pop seemed as calmly impassive in his triumph as he had been in defeat. The two newcomers to the town where they would live for three years (Westfield would never seem like home to Paul as Princeton had been and Somerville would be) grew even closer together. As they had done in Princeton, the old man and the boy spent many evenings together in the parlor, playing checkers—a game that the old man loved. They would play for hours with little talk but a warm sense of companionship.

It was in Westfield that there occurred the one instance Paul could recall when he had disobeyed his father. It was a crucial event to him, and on two occasions he published an account of that boyhood transgression and its lasting effect on him.

> I remember . . . he told me to do something. I didn't do it, and he said, "Come here." I ran away. He ran after me. I darted across the road. He followed, stumbled and fell. I was horrified. I hurried back, helped Pop to his feet. He had knocked out one of his most needed teeth. I shall never forget my feeling. It has remained ever present. As I write, I experience horror, shame, ingratitude, selfishness all over again. For I loved my Pop like no one in all the world. I adored him, looked up to him, would have given my life for him in a flash—and here I had hurt him, had disobeyed him.
>
> Never in all his life (though this was in 1908 and I was ten; he died in 1918) did he have to admonish me again. This incident became a source of tremendous discipline which has lasted until this day [April 1952].[7]

There were too few blacks in that town to allow for a segregated public school, which was the general pattern in New Jersey, and in Westfield Paul attended school with white children for the first time. His relationship with his white classmates was peacefully uneventful. Paul was a big boy, always the largest in his class, and strong and agile—obviously not one to be bullied. "Bunny" Gordon, one of his black schoolmates, remembered Paul as a very good athlete who was well liked by all the children, never got into any fights, never used any bad language, and had a very strict father. Gordon, interviewed when he was a seventy-seven-year-old retired postal worker in New York, shook his head sadly as he recalled the meager lunches that he and Paul took to school: "Nothing but two little old slices of bread, with butter and sugar."[8]

Hard times was all the time at the Robeson parsonage. Though Rev. Robeson was an "excellent financier," his former Princeton congregation had also noted that his "sympathy reached out to all sufferers and in his efforts to give needed relief . . . he often suffered himself in consequence."[9] But despite his poverty-level income William Robeson's children did not feel impoverished, as his daughter Marian, who spent her summer vacations at home, explained:

> As short as the money was, I never remember us going hungry. Pop always had a garden and we ate good. He was always too kind*—to us and everybody. One time there was a doll I saw that I wanted. I think it was one dollar, or sometimes I think it was three dollars, but the one dollar keeps coming to mind. A dollar was a lot of money in those days, and for my father it was even more. When I asked him could I have that doll, he said, no—I should try to do without it. But you know what? That really must have bothered him and he got me that doll! He really took care of us.
>
> As I was saying, Pop was too kind. There was this preacher who wasn't doing too well and Pop would have him come once in a while to preach the sermon [and get the collection]. And this preacher would come on Saturday morning, for breakfast. Imagine, coming *Saturday* morning to preach a sermon! [Question: Your father didn't mind?] Not Pop—*I* was the one that didn't like it. For him, the more the merrier.
>
> There were always a lot of people at the table.[10]

And for the poor pastor's son, Paul, there was the richness of a happy boyhood. Life was fun. School was fun. And play—that was the main fun. Because his lessons came easy to him, Paul would quickly finish his homework and dash out to play baseball, football, or anything else that came to mind. The cry of "Who wants to play?" would always bring Paul running, and he would play until it was too dark to see. The only cloud in his sunny life was the rule that a good boy helped with the chores, and arms that could swing a baseball bat were also expected to wield a rug beater on the parlor carpet hung on the backyard clothesline. Such outdoor chores were not too painful to Paul because quitting time could be set by his own permissive conscience; but he hated all indoor tasks. His hands, so quick and sure in scooping up a bad hop at shortstop (and on the rough playing field of the corner lot nearly all ground balls would bounce erratically), seemed hopelessly awkward at work in the kitchen. "He acted," said his sister— and it must have been one of his most persuasive bits of acting—"as if he never could learn how to wash the dishes, though of course he had to do them when I wasn't home."

---

* To persons acquainted with William Robeson's gentle and retiring daughter that trait of being "too kind" was seen as the most outstanding characteristic of Marian herself.

(That aversion to any kind of household work would be cultivated throughout Paul's life; and in the film version of the musical comedy *Show Boat*, Paul's own feelings on the subject were expressed by the character he portrayed, who in his song "I Still Suits Me" scornfully rejects his nagging wife's complaint that he never does the dishes or any other domestic chores.)

When Paul's brothers Bill and Ben and his sister, Marian, were home from school, the family members frequently entertained themselves with parlor performances rather than with games. (For one thing, card playing was then frowned upon in truly Christian homes: Whist playing could lead to gambling, which led straight to Hell.) In an account of those days written when Ben was the Rev. B. C. Robeson, a prominent Harlem clergyman, it was Bill who first discovered that Paul had a talent for singing. The discovery was said to have been made one day at the parsonage when the three brothers were singing popular ballads in harmony: "We were making one of those minors known only to homeloving groups; Paul was bearing down on it with boyish glee; in fact, all of us were. Out of all the discord, Bill yelled: 'Wait a minute, hit that note again, Paul.' Paul hit it out of the lot [the baseball expression for a home run still came naturally to the former boyhood baseball star], and Bill said: 'Paul, you can sing.'"[11] Paul ridiculed the idea at first, but at Bill's insistence he began to sing with the church choir and at their home performances. Ben recalled: "Entertainments were always numerous, and the law of the parsonage was that every child must do something. The rest of us had recourse to nothing but a recitation or essay, and Paul, to be different, was forced to sing."

Paul Robeson remarked upon the important influence of that home environment at the time of his greatest success in the American theater. Observing that he had been "appearing before audiences since I was eight—in Sunday school and in my father's church," he told an interviewer in 1944:

> My interest in language goes back to my childhood. . . . From my earliest days I have been conscious of the potentialities of the voice to interest, entertain, and particularly to move people deeply. I was brought up in a *vocal* household. My father was the finest speaker I have ever heard. My brothers were all fine, experienced public speakers. In my home, all through my childhood we "orated," recited, or debated. With the single exception of my sister, we all belonged to debating teams in grade, high school and college. We all "tried out" our speeches at home before the highly critical audience of the family.[12]

Paul's homegrown beginnings as a singer, orator, and athlete would first come to public attention in Somerville, New Jersey, where his father was transferred in 1910. That town, about fifteen miles from Princeton, had a more numerous black population than Westfield, and a larger congregation was enrolled in the St. Thomas A.M.E. Zion Church in Somerville, where William Robeson would serve his last pastorate. The parsonage there would be Paul's home through high school and college.

Paul first became noticed by the townspeople when he was still in grade school. (He finished part of seventh grade when he came to Somerville, and that fall he began his last year of grammar school.) As it happened, the pride of each town in the area rested on the success of the local high school baseball team in the fiercely fought contests with the enemy (not merely rival) teams. That Paul was a pupil in Somerville's "colored school" (there were enough of his color in town to have a separate grade school) and not yet a student at the racially integrated high school, was conveniently overlooked. As a good ball player he was "drafted" to help the town's high school in its crucial battles against the other towns, whose players and fans would never suspect that the big black kid at shortstop was not yet in high school.

Within a year of his arrival in town there appeared what must have been Paul Robeson's first press notice. The item, which demonstrated that he had indeed learned early "the potentialities of the voice to . . . move people deeply," was published in a Somerville newspaper when Paul, age thirteen, graduated from the eighth grade.

Colored School Commencement

The closing exercises of the local colored school were held Friday evening [June 23, 1911] in the St. Thomas A.M.E. Zion Church.

The graduates were Paul Leroy Robeson, Margaret Frances Potter and Elsie Victoria Rogers.

The oratorical efforts would well have graced any high school stage, and so impressive were the speakers that many tears were in evidence. To Paul Robeson belongs the credit of a rendition whose excellence has seldom been surpassed by a public school pupil.[13]

Margaret (Potter) Gibbons, who would also graduate with Paul from high school, would not later recall the subject of her own oration on that long-ago summer day in the church where Rev. Robeson was pastor and her mother was the organist.[14] But she was certain nearly sixty years later that Paul's rendition on that occasion was Patrick Henry's famous speech.

If the Muse of Drama would have been pleasantly surprised to see that the earnest young orator could move an audience to tears with such shop-worn material, the Muse of History would have pondered the irony involved: That impassioned appeal for freedom, voiced in 1775 by a white slaveholder in Virginia, now in 1911 stirred the hearts of the people assembled in Somerville's black church, whose slave-born pastor listened with quiet pride as his youngest son declaimed: *I know not what course others may take, but as for me, give me liberty or give me death!*

PART TWO

Li'l David

Li'l David was a shepherd boy,
He killed Goliath and he shouted for joy,
Li'l David play on your harp,
Halleloo, halleloo,
L'il David play on your harp,
Halleloo!

—from a Negro spiritual arranged by Lawrence Brown and sung
by him in duet with Paul Robeson

5

High School: The Fledgling Hero

ON ONE MEMORABLE OCCASION at Somerville High School, Shakespeare's *Julius Caesar* was a tragedy only to Miss Mandel, the teacher in charge of a student performance of the funeral scene of that play. To the assembled student body it was the comedy hit of the year. The two principals were letter-perfect in their roles: Brutus (a white Roman) was played by Doug Brown, captain of the debating team, and Mark Antony (evidently an African Roman) was Paul Robeson, another member of the debating team and the school's champion orator. After speaking his piece to the crowd in the Forum and seeing Antony and others enter, bearing on a stretcher the covered body of the slain Caesar, the noble Brutus urged all to stay and hear Antony's eulogy—"not a man depart, / Save I alone, till Antony have spoke." As he exited, Brutus-Brown struggled to keep from grinning at what would follow.

Then it was Antony-Robeson's turn—to bury Caesar and not to praise him, and so on. Most intent of those who lent the orator their ears was Miss Mandel, who followed each of the well-worn words like a nun counting off her rosary beads, and silently prayed that all should go well. And all did go beautifully as Paul went through the speech, so well rehearsed at home with Pop, and came to the part where Antony, warning his hearers to prepare to shed tears, leans over the corpse to reveal the fatal stab wounds that brought great Caesar low. "And, as he [Brutus] pluck'd his cursed steel away, / Mark how the blood of Caesar follow'd it"—then with a Shakespearean flourish, Paul swept away the covering mantle and there was Caesar's body, white as a sheet (which is what it was, a sheet wrapped around a bundle of rags) and with each of the numerous wounds overflowing with the reddest of gore. At the gruesome sight, Miss Mandel loudly gasped her dismay (there had been no blood at the dress rehearsal) and then the auditorium exploded. Never had an audience at Somerville High been so moved by a classic drama, though the tears that were shed were tears of uproarious laughter as the assembled teenagers howled and clapped and screamed their delight at the sensational practical joke played on the teacher. In her own production it was Miss Mandel and not Julius Caesar who had suffered "the most unkindest cut of all."

The real-life Brutus and Antony, who coconspired to brighten that somber scene with tomato catsup, were close friends during their four years as classmates; and each would remember the other as a brilliant student. Doug Brown became the distinguished Dean J. Douglas Brown, who in retirement after twenty-one years as provost and dean of faculty at Princeton University* recalled with youthful enjoyment that student prank of more than fifty years earlier.[1]

Doug and Paul were two of the eight members of their class who were enrolled in the college preparatory course, which included four years each of Latin and English, three years of German, and four years of mathematics, as well as chemistry, physics, and ancient history. The demanding curriculum was just what Rev. Robeson wanted for Paul, who would become used to Pop's regular query, "Well, son, how did you do in Latin today?" Most of the students (a little more than 200 were enrolled in the school) could not hope to go to college: Their parents could not afford the expense, and most high school graduates were expected to go to work and help support their families until they themselves got married. Paul, of course, was bound for college—there was never a question about that; and it was thought just as certain that the school would be Lincoln University, of which Pop and brother Bill (1902, cum laude) were alumni.

Bill, whom his brothers and sister considered the brainiest of the young Robesons, was frequently at home during those years and shared with Pop the role of home tutor for Paul. The townspeople said that Bill was a "character," meaning somewhat eccentric, and indeed Rev. Robeson's oldest son was more like a character in a Chekhov play than what a young

---

* Dean Brown was also one of the architects of the federal social security system set up during President Franklin D. Roosevelt's administration. He was chairman of the national Advisory Council on Social Security, 1937–1938, and a member of succeeding councils.

black man was expected to be like in Somerville. For one thing, Bill's profession seemed to be that of permanent student: Year after year he would be away at school and then come home during vacation time or periods between the several schools he successively attended.

Circumstances as well as his own inclination made Bill the perennial student. A lack of money had caused him to drop out of medical school at Penn, which he had entered after graduating from Lincoln; and then after supporting himself by working as a Pullman porter and a railroad station redcap,* he began again at a medical college in Boston. However, after graduating from that school, Bill was dismayed to learn that he was not qualified to practice medicine in New Jersey or New York because the Boston school was not accredited elsewhere. For Bill, there was only one thing to do: start all over again at yet another medical school. Finally, in 1921, at the age of 39, and after four years of study at Howard University College of Medicine in Washington, D.C., William D. Robeson Jr. was awarded his long-sought M.D.

More interested in theory than in practice, Bill was seen by many as an indolent person because of his unconcern with making money or being a success. (Paul, who later would sadly note that Bill somehow had not fulfilled his potential—Pop's sole criterion of personal success—thought that Bill's analytical and inquiring mind should have been applied to scientific research work.) Bill's lack of interest in material things was reflected in his indifference to outward appearances. ("Don't say I said it," said a black friend of Bill's who had achieved some prominence in his field, "but the fact is Bill never dressed like a respectable man—more like one of these hippie-types you see nowadays.") That ahead-of-his-times hippie may have influenced his youngest brother's attitude concerning attire, for apart from the requirements of public life Paul would be notably unconcerned with matters of dress. However, Bill's main influence on young Paul, who greatly admired his brother's ability to solve a difficult problem or clarify an abstruse subject, would emerge during Paul's maturity, when his only buying sprees would be in bookstores and his principal spare-time activity would be endless hours of concentrated study.

---

* Many black doctors, lawyers, educators, ministers, and other professionals of Bill's generation and later were helped through college by the black foremen (termed "chiefs") of railroad station porters, who made it a practice to recommend black students for redcap jobs during summer vacations. Proud of their role in thus helping aspiring young blacks to become a "credit to the race," the chiefs viewed any college "drop-out" as one who had failed his people and hence unworthy for any further work as a redcap.

But during his high school years no one thought of Paul as being a studious type. His achievement of the A's his father expected from him was the result of his quickness of mind and the skilled tutoring he got at home rather than from being a bookworm. As in grammar school his main interest was in sports, and here, too, he had encouragement and help at home. Happily, Pop, his mentor and guide, had a high appreciation not only for the Homer of classical literature but for the homer that could win a ball game. Rev. Robeson became such a fixture as a sideline rooter for Paul's teams through high school and college that his son's teammates came to believe that the presence of the old preacher was an augury of victory. Similarly, the admired intellectual brother Bill not only tutored Paul in Latin conjugations but also spent many hours on the playing field coaching Paul in the fundamentals of football. The private coaching was important in giving Paul a good start toward his later national stardom at the game, for Somerville High had no regular football coach; that post was filled at times by the manual training teacher (who according to Doug Brown "didn't know too much about the game") and at other times by the black principal of the Colored School—James L. Jamison (Lincoln, '79), who knew a little more.

Stanley M. Douglas, one of the half-dozen black students in Somerville High (Stanley was one year behind Paul, and his brother Winston was one year ahead), recalled that Paul never seemed to crack a book and was out playing ball every day till dark.[2] That constant practicing plus his natural talent for sports—he was strong, tall and loose-limbed, keen of eye, quick of hand, and light and fast on his feet—made him the school's outstanding player on the football, basketball, and baseball teams. According to Stanley Douglas, when Paul as a grade school ringer played shortstop on the high school baseball team, "He was somewhat awkward, but very effective"; and later, as a catcher—Paul's regular position when he got into high school—"He was excellent." Stanley said that in some of the intercity baseball games Paul became a target for verbal racist abuse and threats of physical violence. In one game against High Bridge (which fortunately for Paul was played in Somerville), "When Paul hit a triple, the principal of High Bridge ran out onto the field hollering, 'That coon didn't touch second!' Well, that caused quite a ruckus, but the Somerville fans rushed out and helped his team protect Paul from being mobbed by the visiting players."

Doug (Brutus) Brown, a teammate of Paul's on the football squad as well as on the debating team, remembered that racial hostility against Paul was also demonstrated by some football opponents:

Paul was usually at fullback, and he was a tremendous player—he was 90 percent of our team. When I was playing halfback and blocked ahead of him, I was more worried about him hitting me in the rear than I was about the opposing team. . . . The hardest game in many ways was with Phillipsburg, where there was race feeling and we knew it. And with every scrimmage we were right in there keeping those guys from hurting Paul—not only because of Paul, but because, too, he *was* our team.*

Paul's interest in athletics led him to serve as sports editor of the school's monthly magazine, which in one unhappy report (it is not known if Paul was the writer) revealed that the Somerville nine had come very close to winning while losing 12 to 0:

Our baseball team was defeated by Plainfield High School by a score of 12-0. The worst of it was, the defeat might easily have been a victory. Plainfield made two hits and scored 10 runs in the first inning. After that things began to brighten up. Three times we thought we had scored, but the umps thought otherwise, and unfortunately for us, our opinions were not considered.[3]

Football, basketball, baseball, and sports editor were not enough for the boundless energy of Rev. Robeson's teenage son. He was also a member of the debating team, sang with the glee club, and acted with the drama group. Then too he sang in the church choir and regularly attended church Sunday school (naturally required of the pastor's son). Occasionally, when Rev. Robeson was ill or out of town, one or another of his sons would deliver the Sunday sermon; and several times while he was in high school and college Paul served as substitute preacher. He did not remember the subject of any of those preachments, but his sister, Marian, laughingly recalled that some of the elderly church members said they looked forward to an early return of the pastor to his pulpit and would mutter about those Robeson boys—going out a-dancing on Saturday (a sin sure enough) and then standing up in church a-preaching on Sunday morning!

---

* In one of the final games—against their chief rival, Bound Brook, Paul suffered a broken collarbone when he was tackled; but the injury was not seen as the result of unsportsmanlike conduct.

There were, however, no complaints but only community pride in Paul's public speaking as a member of the school debating team that was captained by Doug Brown.* The lineup for the team was, first, Doug (lead-off man, to present the basic argument); then a girl, Miriam McConaughy (to develop the case), and finally Paul (cleanup man, to summarize the case and handle the rebuttal).

In the debates, appeals to sentiment were not supposed to be made; only facts and logic were to be employed—"but you couldn't keep Paul from appealing to sentiment," Doug recalled. And he gave an example from their senior year when the question to be debated in the intercity competition was whether immigrants should be required to pass a literacy test. In the contest with Bound Brook, the Somerville team upheld the negative. In his rebuttal Paul graphically depicted the plight of refugees from hunger and tyranny abroad and denounced as heartless the idea of turning away for a lack of education those "tired, poor and huddled masses yearning to breathe free." The audience was moved to tears. "Well, we won that debate hands down," Doug remembered. "But unfortunately the next debate was with Bernardsville and we had to take the other side. We lost."

Happily for Paul's later career in the performing arts, there were several teachers at Somerville High who took a special interest in helping him develop the use of his voice in drama and song and who inspired him and the others to do their best. Fifty years after his Class of 1915 graduated, other surviving members, such as Margaret (Potter) Gibbons, Douglas Brown, Frank Barnes, and Arthur Van Fleet, would express keen appreciation for the dedication and skill of teachers like Anna Miller (English), Elizabeth Van Fleet Vosseller (Music), Miss Vanderveer (Latin), and Miss Bagg (Science).

Coached in debating and acting by Anna Miller, Paul's first appearance as Othello was in a high school performance. The play itself was not attempted, but Miss Miller produced a skit in which a number of Shakespeare's characters gathered at a health resort and presented themselves in readings from their respective plays. Miss Miller was very pleased with Paul's reading ("Soft you; a word before you go./I have done the state some service, and they know't") and with his careful concern to give each

---

* Starting in high school and continuing through college, Paul Robeson may have set some sort of a record by being the star of many teams and the captain of none. It was simply unthinkable in the United States at that time for a black American to be a captain over whites.

word its due (practiced at home with his perfectionist father). She suggested that Paul ought to think about becoming an actor someday, but Paul was certain that the stage was not for him. (Thirty years later, when he was starring as Othello on Broadway, Robeson remembered Anna Miller: "In high school I had a very fine teacher whose passion was Shakespeare. She communicated that passion to many of her classes, and to me. Under her we analyzed Shakespeare's plays, including *Othello*, and thoroughly understood them.")[4]

Whatever racial prejudices they may have had, his teachers responded warmly to the earnest enthusiasm of the gifted black youth who was that rarity—a prize pupil (teacher's pet) and an outstanding athlete (students' hero). Miss Vosseller, a dynamic teacher of music appreciation, urged Paul to join the glee club, which she conducted and taught to sing such oratorios as Handel's *Messiah*. Like his brother Bill, Miss Vosseller insisted that Paul should take seriously his talent for singing. (Doug Brown, who said that Paul was *the* football team, also was with his black classmate in the glee club, where "When Paul cut loose, the rest of us in the bass section just had to wiggle our mouths.") As Paul remembered, Miss Vanderveer, another instructor, seemingly had no taint of racial prejudice, and her Latin class no doubt also helped instill in Paul his lifelong passion for language studies.

Warmly remembered, too, was the science teacher, Miss Bagg, who deeply impressed Paul by her sincerity in urging him to attend the school's social functions, of which she was in charge. For the most part he declined to come to the dances. (Interracial socializing was generally considered by whites to be degrading and was avoided by blacks for fear of disagreeable incidents.) But when he did come, Miss Bagg (who a half-century later might still be deemed ahead of her time) would try to break the ice by being the first to dance with him.

It was in Somerville that Paul first began freely to associate with white people. Though there was a larger than usual black population in the town (of 13,600 residents, 1,400 were black), there were only a few other black students in the school. Two of them, Aaron Johnson and Winston Douglas, played on the football team with Paul. But in most of his activities Paul was a racial minority of one, and that too was "college preparation" for him, as he would enter a college that had not one other black student enrolled. His popularity in Somerville High and among the townspeople opened the doors of many white homes to him. He was the respected black pastor's son; he was unfailingly well mannered; he would readily help another with his homework, and he was the sort of companion parents thought might set a good example for their own teenagers. But more important was Paul's personality, which evoked affection. More than anything else about him his classmates recalled that he was "amiable," "genial," "always nice to everybody—colored or white, it made no difference," and "had no meanness in him—nothing like that"; indeed, "everybody liked him a lot."

Leslie Kershaw, who was a boy soprano in the glee club and a teammate of Paul's in football and basketball, recalled that "All of us were Paul's friends at school as well as after school. He was entertained and dined at all our homes. Everybody's mother was crazy about him and was always holding him up as an example of what they would like us to be. We all felt Paul to be our superior, but we didn't resent it, he was such a great guy."[5]

A devoted fan of the high school hero was a small boy who lived at 80 West Cliff Street, across the street from No. 81, the parsonage of the St. Thomas A.M.E. Zion Church and the home of Rev. Robeson and his family. (Somehow the parsonage, the Colored School that stood next to it at the corner of Davenport Street, and the church on the other side of Davenport had been erected in an otherwise all-white neighborhood.)

Paul's youthful admirer, who suffered the misfortune of being four years younger than his hero and hence unable to be on the high school baseball team with him, was Sam Woldin, whose father, Barnett Woldin, a Jew, was an immigrant from Russia. The senior Woldin, who owned a shoe store, became friendly with his black neighbors; and when he learned that Rev. Robeson had found the land behind the parsonage unsuitable for gardening, the merchant offered the use of his own uncultivated backyard for that purpose. Consequently, as the pastor's beans, cucumbers, and tomatoes ripened in the Woldins' yard, so did the friendship between the heads of the neighboring households. On many summer evenings Sam would see the two old men sitting and talking together on the front porch of his home. And no doubt sometimes they talked about the bond they had in common as refugees from oppression—one from slavery and the lynch terror of Bourbon rule in the South, and the other from the ghetto segregation and pogrom terror of Czarist rule in Russia.

But old men's talk did not interest young Sam, who would tag along after the big boy, Paul, play catch with him, get on a team with the great one in a pickup game in the playground, and never miss a chance to cheer Paul on in games against rival towns. Though Sam was as small for his age as Paul was large for his, he dreamed that someday he too would play for Somerville High. And so he did when he grew older, though not much bigger; and long after, Samuel Woldin, a retired accountant, five-feet-four and going on seventy, recalled with modest pride a glowing moment that came to him. One day the visiting Paul Robeson, then a famous All-American football star, was chatting with Sam and then turned to another who had joined them and said: "Here's the young fellow who filled my shoes at shortstop for Somerville High."[6]

The affection that many white people of the town felt for Paul did not extend to blacks in general (the neighborliness of the Woldins was quite exceptional), and the black and white residents of the small town lived in two separate worlds. The existence of the Jim Crow grammar school and the small number of black students in the high school reflected the inferior economic and social position of the black tenth of the population.

Nor did racism leave Paul untouched. Whereas his classmates recalled that the popular black student had been liked by all who knew him, Paul himself recalled a notable exception. The others would remember Dr. Ackerman, the high school principal, as having a rather dour personality, but Paul remembered the principal as a man who hated him. Each achievement that he gained seemed to increase that official's hostility, and the more popular Paul became with the teachers and student body, the more hateful Dr. Ackerman acted toward him. And it was only over the principal's strenuous objection that Miss Vosseller made Paul soloist for her singing group.

Dr. Ackerman's attitude came as a confusing shock to Paul, who had been certain that all would go well for him in school as long as he "acted right" and measured himself solely in terms of his own potential rather than against others. Modesty was a virtue that came easy to Paul's unassuming nature, but he also knew that modesty was a necessity for the survival of an achieving African American, who must under no circumstances appear to be brash or "uppity." Obeying all the rules—including the unwritten ones called "acting right"—Paul wondered why his efforts to be a "credit to the race" by excellent performance had aroused the animus of the white man in charge. He would learn in time the answer to that seeming contradiction, just as one of his Bustill ancestors had learned it. That forebear was his grandfather Charles's cousin, Sarah M. Douglass, who left the Society of Friends in protest against segregated seating at the meetings. In 1837, reporting that race prejudice had not diminished among the white Quakers of Philadelphia, she wrote: "I have heard it frequently remarked and have observed it myself, that in proportion as we become intellectual and respectable, so in proportion does their disgust and prejudice increase."[7]

At any rate, Paul deeply resented that the principal "never spoke to me
except to administer a reprimand, and he seemed constantly to be looking for an excuse to do so. . . . [Then] his sharp words were meant to
make me feel as miserably inferior as he thought a Negro was." And as a
consequence the genial student expressed for the first time some rebellious thoughts:

> One time he [Dr. Ackerman] sent me home for punishment. Usually Pop
> preferred that the teacher's hand rather than his own should administer the
> proper penalty, but this time I had something to say about that. "Listen,
> Pop," I said, "I'm bigger now. I don't care what *you* do to me, but if that hate-
> ful old principal ever lays a hand on me, I swear I'll try my best to break his
> neck!" I guess Pop understood. He let it go at that.[8]

No matter who might think Paul was an inferior person because of his
race, he himself had every reason not to think so. There was the row of
A's on his report card and the high regard of his teachers, but more important was the judgment of his peers. His schoolmates admired him as
much as they liked him. Thus Douglas Brown, whose later academic
achievements fulfilled his own bright promise as a gifted student, would
look back and say: "It was a rich experience to have four years in school
with as great a human being as Paul—to have him as a warm and loyal
friend; to have him as a fellow student who was already showing the brilliance of genius as an all-around athlete, as a debater, as a singer, and as
an actor, and who could, at the same time, make one push very hard to
keep up with him in a tough academic course."[9]

Nor could Paul believe that his people were an inferior race, though
that idea was dogma for most white Americans.* The notion that their
former enslavement was proof that African Americans were inherently
inferior could make no sense to Paul, whose closest association from his
earliest memory was with the former slave who was his father—the per-

---

* A typical expression of that prevailing doctrine, published when Paul Robeson was a
freshman in high school, came from a noted white historian (a New Englander, not a
Southerner), Hubert Howe Bancroft, who wrote: "However horrid the crime of human
slavery . . . the fact remains that the negro was never so well off, so happy and contented
as when he was the chattel of the chivalrous south. . . . He depends upon the white man
to do his mental work, his thinking and managing for him, preferring himself only to
serve. He is by nature and habit a servant, not alone because of his long period of enslavement, but because of his mental inferiority." See Hubert Howe Bancroft, *Retrospec-
tion* (New York: Bancroft Co., 1912, pp. 370–371, 374).

son whom he most loved and respected. Indeed, it was from that former slave that Paul first learned to scorn the doctrine that the white race was superior to the others. "Just as in youth," he wrote of his father, "he had refused to remain a slave, so in all the years of his manhood he disdained to be an Uncle Tom. From him we learned, and never doubted it, that the Negro was in every way the equal of the white man. And we fiercely resolved to prove it."[10]

The knowledge, gained early in life, that his race was not inferior made it possible for Paul to be at ease with his white classmates and their families. And because he felt good about himself, his family, and his people, his acceptance by whites did not cause him to pull away from associations in the black community. On the contrary, his involvement in the activities of his father's congregation put him in the very center of African American life in the town, of which the church was the main institution. Margaret (Potter) Gibbons, who graduated with Paul from the Colored School in 1911 and was the only other black student graduating with him from high school in 1915, recalled that although most of Paul's teammates in school were white boys, "Whenever the colored boys [nonstudents] got up a team and wanted Paul to play on it, he would always do so."[11]

When at fourteen he finished his freshman year at Somerville High, Paul got his first experience in an area of black American life that had none of the soaring inspiration of choir-singing or the warm conviviality of church socials and picnics. That summer he went to work. Each year Professor Jamison (the principal of the Colored School was always given that title by the community) would take a group of black students for vacation-time work at the resort hotels at Narragansett Pier in Rhode Island. Paul's brother Ben, who had done that work in earlier years, went along on Paul's first venture beyond the small-town world of Somerville, Westfield, and Princeton. Ben was going on twenty and for the previous ten years—since the death of their mother—had been away, except for summers, at high school and then Biddle University (now Johnson C. Smith) in Charlotte, North Carolina.

Kitchen boy was the bottom job in the resort hotel, and on that job Paul was put to work. He who had mumbled and grumbled and dropped dishes and pans in the parsonage kitchen to show his skeptical sister that he was unsuited for washing dishes now came to learn what kitchen-work really was like. He toiled from four o'clock in the morning until after dark, each and every day. And there was twice as much work on Sunday, when the mountain of greasy pots and pans grew even higher. Paul scoured the pots, peeled the potatoes, took out the garbage, scrubbed the work tables, and mopped the floors. And everybody gave him orders—from the chef down to the busboys, who told him as they rolled in their cartloads of dirty dishes, "Hey, country boy, get a move on!" In the steaming heat of those endless midsummer days, Paul must have felt like the sinner-man of whom he would sing in the spiritual "No Hiding Place." That sinner, in Hell, sought the shelter of a rock, but

> the rock cried out, "I'm burning too,
> "I want to go to Heaven as well as you!"
> There's no hiding place down there!

From time to time Ben, who was one of the lordly waiters, would look in upon that fallen innocent from the world of carefree boyhood and give him an encouraging nod. Ben's presence was the only sunshine in Paul's life that summer at the seashore.

In later college years, when Paul returned to Narragansett Pier for summer work (but never again, thank God, as kitchen boy), he made friends with many other black students working their way through school. (He would meet them later still as members of the black professional class.) When he got into the higher ranks of the menials, Paul could join Ben and the others in after-work baseball games against teams from other hotels. At baseball, Ben was the acknowledged star, and the sportswise waiters said that if professional baseball did not have a color bar, Ben would be a cinch to make the big leagues. Ben, however, was set on becoming a minister, and like his father he hoped that Paul, too, would choose that calling.

Sometimes Paul thought that he would be a preacher, as people said he ought to be. People also said that he ought to be a lawyer, since he was so good at debating. But for the most part Paul did not bother to think about what his future might be, and that unconcern would remain throughout his life as a central aspect of his character. His disinclination to make plans for the future even on a short-term basis (which later would sorely vex persons involved in his affairs) was seen in his early years as merely the usual preoccupation of youth with the carefree present. Then too Paul learned early the folk wisdom of his people in the South, who when making a statement about the future—"I'll see you next week"—habitually added the qualification, "if I live and nothing happens."

Something did happen to Paul's long-cherished plan of following Pop and Bill to Lincoln University: The State of New Jersey offered several four-year scholarships as prizes in a statewide competition among high school graduates, and the winners would attend Rutgers College in New Brunswick, New Jersey. Paul was one of the winners of that examination, which was held on June 4 and 5, 1915, during his senior year at Somerville. He regretted that he would not be able to go to Lincoln, but he knew that it would be better for his father to be relieved of the financial burden of sending him there.

(Later, when he wrote about winning the scholarship to Rutgers, Paul noted that he had been compelled to make an extraordinary effort in preparing for the examination. The first part of the test, covering the first three years of high school work, had been held the previous year; but somehow Paul had not known about it then. Consequently, as he recalled, "I was faced with an examination embracing the entire four-year course, in the same three-hour period during which the other competitors would cover only their senior year's work."[12] "Well, I won," he wrote, but with characteristic modesty he chose not to tell his readers the extent of that triumph. Despite the handicap, he passed the examination with the highest average ever achieved in that competition.[13]

During his senior year Paul was also a winner in a statewide competition of high school orators. Though his third-place finish was a disappointment to Paul and his family and friends, in later years he would marvel that he was given any prize at all considering what he said and where he said it. He chose to recite an oration that had been made during the Civil War by the noted white abolitionist Wendell Phillips. The speech was a tribute to Toussaint L'Ouverture, the black liberator of Haiti from the rule of Napoleonic France; and Phillips, noting that Toussaint had been a "pure-blooded African," lauded him as being superior to the greatest white heroes of all time.

You think me a fanatic tonight [Paul declaimed], for you read history not with your eyes, but with your prejudices. But . . . the Muse of History will put Phocion for the Greek, Brutus for the Roman, Hampden for England, Fayette for France, choose Washington as the bright consummate flower of our earlier civilization, and John Brown the ripe flower of our noonday, then, dipping her pen in the sunlight, will write in the clear blue, above them all, the name of the soldier, the statesman, the martyr—Toussaint L'Ouverture![14]

That oratorical contest was held on the campus of Rutgers College, and it is understandable that the judges at the all-white school were not overly pleased to hear the fiery radicalism of Wendell Phillips voiced by the young black orator.

Paul's choice of subject for his recitation did not reflect any radical thinking on his part, for his views were no different from those prevailing in the black community. African Americans were still loyal to the Republican Party, though their faith that the Grand Old Party would bring the Jubilee had long since died. The two pillars on which their hopes rested were the Church (for spiritual comfort in this world and the promise of material comfort in the next) and Education (to train those who would lead the race to equality). In retrospect Paul thought it was probably his brother Bill who had suggested he use the famous abolitionist oration, and the surmise seems likely in view of the fact that of all the Robeson children, Bill had had the longest association with their mother, whose Bustill family had been militant abolitionists for generations. (Bill was twenty-three when Maria Louisa died.)

Another antiracist subject was the topic of Paul's speech when the thirty-eight members of his class were graduated from Somerville High School on June 17, 1915. Paul was the last of several student-speakers on the program whose remarks were original compositions, not recitations. His topic, which was "Elijah P. Lovejoy,"* may have been suggested by Rev. Robeson. For one thing, Elijah Lovejoy, an abolitionist newspaper editor who was killed by a proslavery mob, personified a concept that was, as Paul remembered, "the text of my father's life—loyalty to one's convictions. Unbending. Despite everything."[45] Then too it is likely that when William Robeson was studying for the Presbyterian ministry he came to venerate the name of Elijah Lovejoy, who forty years earlier had been graduated as a Presbyterian minister from Princeton's divinity school.

No record exists of Paul's speech on that occasion, but he may have quoted from Rev. Lovejoy's famous open letter, in which the beleaguered antislavery editor noted, "If you give ground a single inch, there is no stopping place" and concluded by saying: "Fellow citizens, they told me that if I returned to the city, from my late absence, you would surely lay violent hands upon me, and many friends besought me not to come. . . . [Nevertheless] I have appeared openly among you . . . I can die at my post, but I cannot desert it."[16]

---

* Elijah Parish Lovejoy (1802–1837), a Presbyterian minister and editor, refused to cease his antislavery crusade even though his newspaper presses were thrice destroyed in Alton, Illinois. On November 7, 1837, a fourth mob attack was made, and despite an armed defense, the press was again wrecked and Rev. Lovejoy shot to death. His martyrdom brought many other Americans into the abolitionist movement.

But the anti-Lovejoy mob attack at Alton, Illinois, was eighty years past, and the anti-Robeson mob at Peekskill, New York, was more than thirty years in the future. At age seventeen the only confrontations Paul Robeson was thinking about were the crunch of one football line against the other, the baseball catcher braced to tag out the runner charging home, and the artful feints of a basketball player against the opposing man.

The winning of the scholarship to Rutgers had determined that he would not play for the school of his father and Bill; but in one respect the workings of Fate, which Paul had not yet come to believe in, made the choice of Rutgers better for Paul as well as for his father. Had he gone to all-black Lincoln instead of all-white Rutgers Paul Robeson would never have been All-American.

❦ 6 ❦

Rutgers 1:
A Long Ways from Home

$\mathcal{I}$T WAS A SHORT TRIP TO THE DIFFERENT WORLD that Paul Robeson entered in the fall of 1915. New Brunswick, where Rutgers College was located, was only about fifteen miles from Somerville, in the direction of his Princeton birthplace. Yet if ever Paul felt "like a motherless child, a long ways from home," it must have been during his first days at Rutgers.

The college, which later became a state university with an enrollment in the tens of thousands, was then a small, private men's college with fewer than 500 students. One of the nation's oldest institutions of higher learning, Rutgers was founded ten years before the Declaration of Independence by well-to-do members of the Dutch Reformed Church who decreed that only an adherent of that ultraconservative branch of Calvinism could be the school's president. The intolerant spirit often attributed to the Dutch Protestant immigrants in America (and later in South Africa) was strongly evident during Robeson's Rutgers years, which would see, for example, a lone student antiwar dissenter brutalized by a campus mob and literally ridden out of college on a rail. And even the off-campus dissent of striking railroad workers would become a matter for repressive action by Rutgers (one of whose trustees was president of the Delaware & Hudson Railway), as noted in an annual report by the college president: "Another interesting item in the life of the year [1919–1920] was the enlisting of students, about 150 in all, in the maintaining of railroad service when strikes threatened to completely break it down. . . . The railroads expressed gratitude to the students and to the college for the service."[1]

Though he was, of course, quite guiltless of any antiwar or pro-labor tendencies at that time, Freshman Robeson was nevertheless an obvious nonconformist in the crucial matter of color. But he had won a state scholarship and Rutgers had to admit him as its only black student.*

He came in like a lamb. He was seventeen and full of innocence. Favorite child of a loving father, smiled upon by congregation and community, teacher's pet and most popular boy in high school—love had made him sweet and gentle. More than anything, he liked to play, and so there must have been a shy smile of anticipation on his smooth brown face as he trotted onto the playing field in his first tryout for the football team. If he knew then that the others on the field—team members from the previous year and the newcomers who hoped to make the team—had attended a two-week preseason training camp at Eatontown to which he had not been invited, the thought would not have bothered the incoming hero from Somerville High. As it said in Pop's Bible, "By their deeds shall ye know them," and Paul was certain that once they saw what he could do he would be more than welcome. Then the truth hit him—with fists and elbows and knees and feet—and Paul's career at Rutgers was almost ended before it had begun.

Years later, when he was starring on Broadway and discussed with a *New York Times* reporter his portrayal of Othello's rage, Robeson would vividly recall the pain and despair that had come crashing down on him as a teenage freshman and the terrible rage that had lifted him to manhood.[2] Recalling that the white boys "—well, they didn't want a Negro on their team, they just didn't want me on it," he told how on that first day of scrimmage they set out to make sure he would not get on the team.

One boy slugged me in the face and smashed my nose, just smashed it. That's been a trouble to me as a singer every day since. And then when I was down, flat on my back, another boy got me with his knee, just came over and fell on me. He managed to dislocate my right shoulder.

Well, that night I was a very, very sorry boy. Broken nose, shoulder thrown out, and plenty of cuts and bruises. I didn't know whether I could take any more. But my father—my father was born in slavery down in

---

* Before coming to Rutgers, Paul had heard that two other blacks had previously managed to attend the school. One of them, a lawyer whom Paul came to know, had graduated before Paul was born; but he never learned what happened to the other one.

North Carolina—had impressed me that when I was out on a football field or in a classroom or just anywhere else I wasn't there just on my own. I was the representative of a lot of Negro boys who wanted to play football and wanted to go to college, and, as their representative, I had to show that I could take whatever was handed out.

During the ten days that he lay in bed recovering from the battering he had taken and trying to decide if he should stay where he was so brutally unwanted, he must have thought about the trials and triumph of his Uncle Frank—Dr. Nathan Francis Mossell, husband of Paul's mother's sister, Gertrude. As the sole black student at the University of Pennsylvania Medical School, Mossell had met with ostracism and physical abuse. An effort was made to compel him to sit behind a screen while in class, and on several occasions students tried to jostle him into the nearby river. But despite the most vicious mistreatment Uncle Frank achieved top grades and gradually won the respect of most of his classmates; and when in 1882 he became the first African American to graduate from that school, "The provost had to ask the students to stop applauding when Dr. Mossell received his diploma."[3]

Most persuasive, perhaps, were the bedside words of Paul's much-admired oldest brother, Bill, who said in a visit to the bandaged youngster: "Kid, if you want to quit school, go ahead, but I wouldn't like to think, and our father wouldn't like to think, that our family had a quitter in it."

"So I stayed," Paul said in that interview with the *Times* writer, and then went on to tell what happened when he went back for his second tryout for the team:

> I made a tackle and was on the ground, my right palm down on the ground. A boy came over and stepped hard on my hand. He meant to break the bones. The bones held, but his cleats took every single one of my fingernails off my right hand.
>   That's when I knew rage!
>   The next play came around my end, the whole first-string backfield came at me. I swept out my arms—like this—and the three men running interference went down, they just went down. The ball-carrier was a first-class back named Kelly. I wanted to kill him and I meant to kill him. It wasn't a thought, it was just a feeling, to kill. I got Kelly in my two hands and I got him over my head—like this. I was going to smash him so hard to the ground that I'd break him in two, and I could have done it.
>   But just then the coach yelled, the first thing that came to his mind, he yelled: "Robey, you're on the varsity!" That brought me around. We laughed about it often later. They all got to be my friends.

As might be expected, some of the other players told a different story many years later when they were asked about Paul's football tryout. Harry J. Rockafeller, a veteran member of the 1915 team and then a college senior, said he was certain that the black freshman had not been mistreated. Rockafeller, who became football coach at Rutgers and was on the selections committee of the Football Hall of Fame that barred Robeson's name from that pantheon of the college game, said he had always thought highly of his former teammate until Robeson turned to "excessive liberalism" later in life.[4] And Kenneth M. ("Thug") Rendell, a teammate of Paul's for three years and captain of the great 1917 eleven, insisted that Robey—the name they all remembered him by—had never been manhandled and indeed had always been treated like a gentleman, which was the way that Robey in turn always treated the others.[5]

Two other teammates, Alfred A. Neuschaefer and William A. Feitner, who were members of Robey's graduation class in 1919, did not deny that their fellow freshman had been roughly treated. But they were sure no racist feelings were involved. Neuschaefer, class historian, did not comment directly on what happened to Robey but instead recalled that he himself had been roughed up by the regulars that fall when he tried out for the team. It was customary, he said, for men on the team to use such tactics to forestall competition for their places.[6]

Least reticent on the subject was Bill Feitner, team captain in 1918 and president of the Class of 1919, who was not one of the players when Robey tried out for the team. He said that the rough treatment was done at the direction of George Foster Sanford, the coach, who saw that the black newcomer had the physical and mental qualities to become a great player. "So Sanford said, 'Now look, let's treat this boy rough, so that he knows he's not as good as he probably thinks he is coming in here.' Which they did. They treated him real rough—not in any way you wouldn't treat in football—but they gave him the works. Then they came to a point where Sandy said, 'Now let's quit. Now we've shown him we've got good players on the team. Let's make Robey that kind of player.'" According to Feitner the treatment had lasting value: "In my humble opinion, it was the thing that made Robey."[7]

It must be doubted, however, that Coach Sanford had ordered the bone-crushing assault that some of the other players would not remember and Robeson could not forget. Sanford, a giant of a man who had played on the legendary Yale football team of 1891 (Yale—490; Opponents—0) together with such immortals as Heffelfinger and Hinkey, would become not only a dedicated mentor to Robey as an athlete but his closest counselor at Rutgers. An example of the coach's fairmindedness was cited by Sanford's son—George F. Sanford Jr.—who recalled that on one occasion when he was a teenager traveling with the team, his father had physically punished a Pullman conductor who sought to eject Robey from the team's coach.[8]

Sanford had been brought to Rutgers two years earlier through the efforts of one of its trustees who was keenly dissatisfied with the school's low standing in college football—a weakness that had persisted since 1869, when Rutgers and Princeton made history by engaging in America's first intercollegiate football match. That trustee, Leanor F. Loree, who was president of the Delaware & Hudson Railway, would soon be gratified to see the scarlet of Rutgers ranked among such prestigious football colors as Harvard's crimson, Yale's blue, and Princeton's orange and black.* By the time Paul Robeson arrived on campus, "Sandy" had fashioned an outstanding squad. The 1915 team, onto which the black freshman had fought his way, went on to win all but one of that year's games.

As it happened, the sole loss—to Princeton's Tigers in the season's second game—would become for Paul the most distressing gridiron defeat suffered by Rutgers during his four years on the team. Not unexpectedly, he did not get to play in that game, for in those years a substitute like Paul usually sat out the game unless the regular player at his position was injured. But to Robey's subsequent chagrin no other football match was played against Princeton while he was at Rutgers, and so he never achieved his dream of helping to inflict a crushing defeat on a Tiger eleven.

Paul's keen desire to meet and beat Princeton soon became known to other students to whom he may have said (as he later remarked to this writer, and only half in jest) that his main reason for joining the Scarlet basketball and baseball teams was to get a chance to play against Princeton. His teammates and the local sports reporters who wrote about Robey's zeal in this matter saw it as a commendable expression of college spirit concerning a rival school; but it was in fact a reflection of the strong feeling in the region's black communities that Princeton University was rabidly antiblack. Not only did Princeton maintain a total ban on black enrollment (except for its divinity school) but its athletic teams were said

---

* Loree's gratification was matched by that of Sanford, whose insurance brokerage business in New York was given the account of Loree's railroad. That arrangement had helped induce Sanford to accept the unsalaried post of football coach at Rutgers.

to use brutal methods against black players on opposing teams. Added to
the prevailing view of his people that Princeton players were so many
Klansmen in athletes' uniforms were Paul's memories of the mistreatment
his family had suffered in the town dominated by that university—Bill's
exclusion from the local high school, Reed's problems with racist students, and above all the Establishment-directed ouster of Rev. William
Robeson from his pulpit. However, because Rutgers was no place for a
lone black student to express resentment against racial injustice, the white
students and reporters knew nothing about the source of Paul's anti-
Princeton attitude. And former teammates like Harry Rockafeller, who
charged that in later years Paul Robeson "turned against his homeland,"
did not notice that the genial Robey they knew in college had in fact
turned against his hometown.

A highlight for Freshman Robey was his attendance in December at
New Brunswick's annual civic banquet for the football team, and he saved
the menu of the dinner at Klein's Hotel as a souvenir. However, somebody
had evidently fumbled the ball by inviting him, and never again would he
attend the town's banquet honoring his team. Because he was black, in the
succeeding years there would be no room for him at the inn, not even
when he became the team's most honored player. As Robey's teammate
and class president Bill Feitner, a retired engineer, explained: "In those
days—and don't forget, that was many years ago—colored people were
not accepted in hotels and public restaurants, and so whenever there was
a banquet for the team, Paul always arranged, gracefully, to have some
other place to go." It was, said Feitner, "a fine thing for him to do."

Racial segregation was not only the rule at off-campus college functions but was practiced within the institution itself. Thus, until the later
enrollment of another black student,* Paul was required to live alone in
Winants Hall, one of the college residences. That circumstance would
later cause one of the white students who knew him to suggest that the
segregated housing may have been a unique advantage for the black student. Earle V. Conover (Rutgers, '20), who remembered Paul as "my
ideal of a college man," speculated that by not having a roommate Robey
"could concentrate on work, whereas most of us were socializing and
hell-raising, wasting time often."[9]

---

* Robert R. Davenport of Orange, New Jersey, entered Rutgers the following year and
became Robeson's roommate and friend on campus and in later years.

Paul did in fact study harder during his freshman year than he did in the succeeding years when he had a roommate, but that was not because he lived alone. In the classroom as on the football field he felt the compelling need to be what his father, his family, and the black communities of Princeton, Westfield, and Somerville expected him to be, namely, A Credit to His Race. That phrase, capitalized like Holy Writ by the solemn tones of those who voiced it, reflected a social dogma that had developed over the fifty years since slavery was overthrown. Subscribed to by nearly all African Americans and by those white persons who wished them well or said they did, the preachment held that any African American who managed to climb above the lowest place must, by his superior performance, be an example of what his people could achieve if they but had the opportunity.

Happily for young Paul, whose natural gifts had made him preeminent in high school, the discriminatory requirement to prove he was an equal by demonstrating superiority was not unduly burdensome. Even in that first year, when he was out to prove that he could be a star in studies as well as in sports, Paul was anything but a bookworm. George A. Kuyper, highest honor student in the Class of 1919, remembered that "during our freshman year, when [Paul] and I spent many hours together" working on study assignments, "he was always in a hurry to get through with the homework."[10]

If his quickness of mind made learning come easy to the aspiring Credit to His Race, Paul's amiable nature ("a tremendous personality, with a hearty laugh, a big, warm smile, a wonderful sense of humor," in Kuyper's recollection) made it easy for him to cope with his exclusion from banquets and other social functions. Robey's tactful pretense of always having something else to do on such occasions—that "fine thing" of never making the others feel uncomfortable because of the pain their racism inflicted on him—was a type of conduct that the black community termed "acting right." Most members of that community agreed with the teachings of Booker T. Washington, the most influential black leader of the time, who said in a famous and often-quoted speech: "The wisest among my race understand that the agitation of questions of social equality is the extremest folly."[11] Though there were some who thought that the worst folly was to practice what Booker T. preached, none among his race would have doubted that for the black minority of one at Rutgers there was no choice but to "act right." If Paul acted wrong he'd soon be long gone.

For the most part, however, Robey had only to act himself to be warmly accepted by his white classmates. As in high school, he was a welcome visitor to the homes of some of them, like that of George Kuyper, who recalled: "The highest moments of our relationship—for me—were the occasions when Paul went home with me for the weekend. My parents went to a very orthodox church (Dutch Reformed). Although I had left that church, whenever I was at home I pleased them by going to church with them. Paul was a good sport and went with us to the Sunday morning services. My parents were quite proud to 'show him off' to our neighbors."

Malcolm S. Pitt, later a dean at Hartford Theological Seminary, had a cooperative study arrangement with the black student: "He helped me with Greek and I used to untangle his trig problems."[12] Robey's friendliness made a lasting impression on J. Harold Thomson, who, a retired Presbyterian minister fifty years later, gratefully recalled how Paul had helped him with Greek. In a letter to this writer, Rev. Thomson wrote: "Tell him too that he is Number Two on my personal 'Hero List.' Number One is Woodrow Wilson! I think he will get a chuckle out of that."[13] (Paul, in fact, was amused and pleased to hear from "Tommy," who had left Rutgers to serve in World War I and had been wounded in France.)

Tutored by some and tutoring others, Robey completed his freshman year with near-perfect marks. Even his father, who earlier had chided Paul whenever his report card showed less than all A's, must have been pleased by his youngest son's initial attainments at Rutgers—seven A's (in English Literature, Greek, English Composition, Public Speaking, Trigonometry, Solid Geometry, and Physical Training) and one B (in Rhetoric). Although he modestly shared Pop's quiet satisfaction with his good start in college (boastful talk, like bad language, was deemed entirely out of place in the Robeson household), Paul's springtime of success had been marred by one distressful failure. The Rutgers baseball team, which Paul had joined, opened its season against Princeton, and, as was traditionally the case in all sports competitions between the longtime rival schools, Rutgers was badly beaten. Paul would have to wait until next winter's basketball season to get another crack at a team from Princeton—that collegiate citadel, as he saw it, of White Supremacy.

Paul was eighteen that spring of 1916. After his successful freshman effort to prove equality by superior performance, he could relax a little and give more time to girls, a developing enthusiasm second only to sports. In Somerville, where church folk viewed dancing and card playing as sinful, a preacher's son had no business messing around with girls. And around

Rutgers in New Brunswick, under the watchful eyes of the white folks, the most decorous conduct was called for. But when Paul went to other towns—to Princeton, Trenton, Philadelphia, Newark, and New York—it was a different story. The prizewinning young spellbinder could turn the heads of the girls who thronged around him at parties, and the love songs he was invariably called upon to sing could melt their hearts.

Among respectable colored people (the only kind the Robesons associated with), "keeping company," as dating was called, was deemed proper only when the young man's intentions were said to be honorable—his only object, matrimony. Every right-thinking young man was expected to settle on one true love whom he would marry when he could support a wife and raise a family. As it happened, the thoroughly conventional young Paul Robeson found his one true love (so he would say) that spring in Freehold, New Jersey, a small town some twenty miles south of New Brunswick. He had gone there to deliver an oration at the Young Men's Christian Association (YMCA), and when he attended a local Sunday school session he met a young woman with whom he soon began to keep company.

Forty years later Paul could not recall the subject of his remarks to that YMCA audience. It was probably not an original speech, he told the writer, but was perhaps some inspirational essay like Elbert Hubbard's "A Message to Garcia" or Rudyard Kipling's "If," which was Paul's favorite poem in college. But as for the young woman he met on that trip, he never forgot her. Her name was Geraldine Neale, and she was a high school student who later became a schoolteacher.

"Gerry—everybody called her Gerry," Paul said, "and everybody knew we were going to be married when we finished school. My family, her people, all our friends—they all knew it. We were meant for each other, everybody said that, too, and I'm as sure of that today as I was back then. Gerry—she was just perfect, so sweet—the one woman in the world for me." Rightly suspecting that his listener, who had been a close friend for years, had doubts he could ever have been a one-woman man, he went on, "Don't laugh when I tell you—and I really mean it—that Gerry would have been the only woman for me through it all. The *only* one!"

In the summer of 1916, Paul left New Jersey for a vacation of hotel work and after-hours plays at Narragansett Pier, where he had first gone from high school to toil unhappily as a kitchen boy. As a college man, he now was employed as a waiter, which gave him a chance to play on the waiters' baseball team in games against other hotels. Not the least of the relaxation for Paul was the change from the all-white world of Rutgers, where he must ever prove the worth of his race, to the all-black society of the Rhode Island resort workers among whom he had to prove nothing.

One of those workers, who became a friend for many years, was Frederick D. (Fritz) Pollard. Several years older than Paul, Fritz was a student at nearby Brown University and was, like Paul, that rarity of the time—a black player on a white football team. The two would play on opposite sides that fall of 1916, which was the year that Pollard was chosen as the second black All-American in football history.*[14]

In his scrapbook that fall Robey listed himself as left tackle on the Rutgers eleven, and as usual he entered the scores of each of their games. How constrained he felt at the school is shown by the fact that when he listed the 13-to-13 tie with Washington and Lee University, he made no mention of the cruelest hurt he suffered at Rutgers.

What happened was this: The game against the team from Washington and Lee (the "Lee" in the name of the Virginia school honors Robert E. Lee, the Confederate Army commander) was scheduled in conjunction with the sesquicentennial celebration of the founding of Rutgers (1766–1916). The visiting Southerners threatened to spoil the festivities by calling off the match unless they were spared the indignity of competing against a player they deemed racially inferior. Rutgers complied with their demand. As Bill Feitner, one of Robey's teammates, blandly recalled: "They refused to play if Robeson played, so since they were in New Brunswick and all other arrangements having been made, there was nothing Sandy [Coach Sanford] could do but concede. I played Robey's position in that game."[15]

The decision to capitulate to the Virginians, which must have been made by officials higher than the coach, evoked a sharp letter of protest to the college from James D. Carr, a New York lawyer who in 1892 had been the first African American to graduate from Rutgers.† Carr, who belatedly

---

* The first was William H. Lewis, who played center at Harvard and was picked by Walter Camp for the All-America teams of 1892 and 1893. Lewis, a lawyer, was at first a radical opponent of Booker T. Washington's policies; but as a consequence of his reconciliation with the powerful black leader, Lewis was appointed an assistant attorney general by President William Taft.

† When Paul Robeson, while attending Columbia Law School, pasted into his scrapbook a newspaper obituary of James Dickson Carr, who died in 1920 at the age of fifty-one, he must have been struck by the similarities in Carr's early life and his own. Like Robeson, Carr was the son of a Presbyterian minister; and like Rutger's second black graduate the first had been an honor student who had won prizes in oratory and election to Phi Beta Kappa at the end of his junior year, and subsequently had graduated from Columbia Law School.

learned of the incident, expressed "deep chagrin and bitterness" that his college had surrendered to "men whose progenitors tried to destroy this Union." He also pointed to what he saw as a larger issue involved in the injustice done to Rutger's sole black student and speculated on how the incident might later affect the aggrieved young man: "Not only he, individually, but his race as well, was deprived of the opportunity of showing its athletic ability, and, perhaps, its athletic superiority. . . . Can you imagine [Paul's] thoughts and feelings when, in contemplative mood, he reflects in years to come that his Alma Mater faltered and quailed when the test came, and that she preferred the holding of an athletic contest to the maintenance of her honor and her principles?"[16]

On the day of the game there was no way for Robey to do the "fine thing" again and pretend he had another engagement elsewhere. As a regular on the team there was nothing for him to do but sit out the match with the subs on the bench and be a spectator at the sporting event from which his color barred him. What his thoughts were that day are not known, but how soul-searing the experience was for the sensitive youngster can be guessed from the fact that in later years, he did not like to hear about it. Unlike the broken bones of his tryout for the team—which he later often talked about, always without rancor—his exclusion from the Washington and Lee game was a wound that never healed.

The incident, which was central to the ambivalence he always felt about Rutgers, no doubt was seen by the anguished Robey as a shocking act of betrayal by his pals on the team and by the coach whom he idolized. As for the racism of the Southerners—grandsons of the class that had enslaved his father—that was something to be expected of "crackers." But when in later years Paul Robeson reflected on the matter, he was not at all concerned, as James Carr imagined he would be, that his alma mater had been faithless to "her honor and her principles." At the heart of his enduring chagrin was this conviction, which grew stronger with time: By "acting right" he had been utterly wrong. When he silently accepted that blatant injustice, he had indeed been true to the concern of his father and his community and his coach that he keep his eyes, no matter how tear-filled at the moment, on the goal of success. But as he came to see it, he told this writer, he had not been true to himself. The glory of the next two years that would come to the fabulous "Robeson of Rutgers" and be for him a lifelong source of prideful memory would never have come to pass had young Robey acted as the mature Paul Robeson thought he should have acted—refused to play another game for Rutgers. The pride and the regret would coexist within him all his days.

Robey never missed another football game at Rutgers. And as it happened, in the very next game that followed the all-white encounter with Washington and Lee, his race took full advantage of the opportunity to show its athletic ability and "perhaps," as James Carr put it, "its athletic superiority." But the hero of that game in Providence, Rhode Island, against Brown University, was not the powerful black giant on the visiting team but the small black speedster who played halfback for Brown. That star was Fritz Pollard, Paul's summertime friend. The game provided Paul with one of his favorite football stories—how the elusively fast, 160-pound Pollard outmaneuvered the Rutgers defense, including big Paul at tackle, and scored all three of Brown's touchdowns. And Pollard, who failed in his studies, would later recall with a chortle: "Just ask Paul— he'll tell you that *I* was the Phi Beta Kappa man on the field that day!"[17] To be remembered in Paul's college book, along with his regret that Rutgers had lost, was the fact that Fritz had arranged a party for him after the game that was attended by a number of pretty girls from Providence. If Paul had not been the star on the field, he plainly was the star attraction that night.

That combination of his two enthusiasms—competing in each season's sports and after-game partying with girls—became such a steady pattern throughout Robey's college years that it is a wonder he maintained a high scholastic standing. Not only did he twice play on four varsity teams in the same school year* but he also managed to find the time—incredible as that might seem—to play on yet another team that was based in New York. That noncollegiate basketball team, the St. Christopher Club, was sponsored by a church in Harlem; and Robey's playing with this all-black, semiprofessional club on Sundays, holidays, and between semesters was of threefold advantage to him. He had another team to play for; he earned extra money from the gate receipts; and the after-game parties in the black communities where "St. C." competed brought swarms of hero-worshiping girls.

Robey variously played guard, center, and forward on the Rutgers basketball team, which was not of the caliber of the Harlem club, a number of whose players later starred as professionals. The Rutgers five not only were not champions but, to Robey's unhappiness, were once again

---

*In his third and fourth years Robeson was a member of the football, basketball, and track teams. As a freshman he played football and baseball; and as a sophomore, football, basketball, and track. Altogether he played on thirteen varsity teams.

trounced, 36-17, by Princeton. He would have to wait until his third year for another try against the hated Tigers.

As for college activities other than sports, Robey was not a member of the glee club as he had been in high school. From the outset the Rutgers singing group had made clear that the black student was not good enough to be one of them. It was not that his baritone was deemed faulty, but the glee club had many social affairs where a black skin would have been considered out of harmony with the others. However, despite that exclusion, Paul's voice was often heard in song performances on the campus and off. As a singer of the popular tunes of the day, Paul also earned extra money by singing at various church and community affairs, his piano accompanist at times being his football teammate Al Neuschaefer.*

Again unlike in high school, Robey had no drama-group activity in college, but his interest in Shakespeare's plays was further developed. As a freshman he listed *Hamlet* as his favorite drama, and his English teacher, like Miss Miller at Somerville High, would be warmly remembered as a helpful influence on his later acting career. That professor was Charles W. Whitman. An authority on Shakespeare, Dr. Whitman, who was Robeson's closest friend on the faculty, took his favorite student to several Shakespearean productions on Broadway, the first of which starred the famous David Warfield in *The Merchant of Venice*. Years later, when he himself was a Shakespearean star on Broadway, Paul recalled the helpfulness of that professor and the deep impression made on him by the actors who used their voices so marvelously and whose diction was so impeccable.

His own voice and diction helped Robey win the sophomore prize for public speaking—the second year he had been best orator in his class. And he also repeated his freshman achievement of being listed as an honor student.

At midpoint in his college career and filled with high spirits and boundless energy, Paul Robeson was poised for his third and most memorable year at Rutgers, when he would reach the top as athlete and scholar and suffer his most grievous loss.

---

* In a message to Paul Robeson in 1971, Neuschaefer, a retired physical education teacher, marveled that he had ever accompanied "the world's greatest artist" and recalled that when Paul performed between the acts of a play at a Newark church the audience did not want the play to resume—they preferred to hear more of Paul's singing.

7

Rutgers 2: "Othello of Battle"

ON APRIL 6, 1917, THREE DAYS BEFORE Paul Robeson's nineteenth birthday, the Virginia-born and Princeton-schooled president of the United States led the nation into the first World War. Woodrow Wilson, a professor at Princeton at the time of Paul's birth in that town and who later as president of the university maintained its ban against the enrollment of black Americans, now summoned all Americans to enroll in his crusade to make the world safe for democracy. To the call for all-out patriotism, usually referred to as "100 percent Americanism," Rutgers, with its long tradition of parochial conformity, responded with a vengeance.

The vengeance was visited upon the only person on the campus who expressed opposition to the war. He was Samuel Chovenson, a freshman scholarship student from Millville, New Jersey. When that singular young man refused, because of his socialist principles, to comply with his professor's requirement that all class members make a pro-war speech, his white skin did not save him from a beating even more brutal than had been inflicted upon the black skin of Robeson. And after he was beaten by a mob of Rutgers students, the dissident was doused with molasses, covered with feathers from several emptied pillows, and carried on a plank through the main streets of New Brunswick. There were shouts of "Lynch him!" and the mob procession that took the war-resister out of town displayed placards denouncing the battered victim as a "pro-German" and one that read: "He's a Bolsheviki."[1]

Robey, who thirty years later would himself be the target of similar shouts from menacing mobs, was not a witness to that scene, which would have terrified any black observer. But later, when he learned what had been done by the campus patriots—including some of his own classmates—he must have reflected that had he been that dissident they surely would have lynched him. Happily for him, however, he had no pacifist principles to put him in peril. The Robesons, like most black Americans, shared the general belief in the righteousness of the war and hoped that the friendly Uncle Sam who now wanted them to join his army would permit them a share of the New Freedom to come.

Paul's nearest-in-age brother, Ben, who was studying for the ministry, would enlist as an Army chaplain for service overseas with a black regiment. But Paul himself was not studying about going to war. Though he would win his third oratorical prize with a pro-war speech, he never considered volunteering for the armed forces as did some of his campus friends. One of them was Harold ("Tommy") Thomson, the lad who was "terrible in Greek" and was tutored by Robey. He enlisted in the infantry and was wounded in action in France. And another was Kenneth Rendell, the 1917 football captain and star performer at tackle, who joined the Navy. But the only uniform Robey wanted to wear was that of an athlete. He would find his glory not in Flanders's fields overseas but on the football fields at home.

When the 1917 football season ended, Paul Robeson was considered by many experts to be the best football player in America. And the following year that consensus became virtually unanimous. Some leading authorities on the sport, like Walter Camp, who was often referred to as the father of American football, judged the black star to be the all-time best at his position.

Though Robey was listed on the team rosters of those years as left end and was twice named All-American at that position, he played only part of the time at end. In many games he also played at left tackle and right tackle and in the backfield. Then too he often had the assignments of being the kickoff man and the punt-receiver as well. That extraordinary one-man "platooning" system,* devised by Coach Sanford to utilize fully Robey's manifold talents, was described by a reporter who noted that "In

---

* Under the so-called platooning system later established in college and professional football, each side uses two teams: One plays only on the offense, the other only on the defense.

our football experience covering twenty-five years, we never have seen a player who approached him in versatile usefulness." He wrote:

> Robeson is nominally classed in Rutger's line-up as an end. But this is only titular. He is everything and everywhere. He is never in the same position in two plays. He is usually on the end, around which the runner sweeps, or if it is an off-tackle thrust or plunge between tackle and guard, he takes a position inside the end. . . . When Rutgers receives a kickoff the tall negro is placed on the 10-yard line just in front of the goal posts, in the best position to take the ball. He catches the ball naturally and gracefully, handling it like a feather. He runs with an amble, his long strides covering ground very fast. While not a skillful dodger, his great strength and weight make him a hard man to stop.[2]

According to that observer, Robeson was also very effective both in catching and in throwing forward passes (the latter ability being especially notable because the football then used was larger and rounder than the more easily grasped football of later years). "As an actor in the forward pass," he wrote, "Robeson plays either role. One pass he made [against a Naval team] carried forty yards. He also took a forward pass from Gardner for a gain of 27 yards."

Another description of Robey's versatility was given by the sports editor of the *Philadelphia Public Ledger,* who came to share the belief of "all of the New York critics" that the black player was "the wonder of the age." Asserting that "Robeson . . . is without doubt the best football player in the country today," he told his readers:

> On the attack he plays end for a time, then shifts to tackle, first on one side and then the other; jumps back of the line on a shift play and at other times stands far out on the end. He is all over and plays against half a dozen men in the course of a game. On the defense he backs up the line, taking the place of a roving center. He looks after line bucks, and runs and is the principal defense against the forward pass. There is nothing he can't do and I believe he is one-half the Rutgers team.[3]

Nearly all newspaper accounts made reference to Robeson's large physique: He was "towering," "gigantic," "Herculean." Though his height and weight—six feet two and one-half inches, 210 pounds—would not be thought remarkable for a football player today, he did in fact tower over his contemporaries. Thus on the 1917 Rutgers team, which was rated among the top three teams in the country, there were only four six-foot-ers among the eighteen other members on the squad, and their average weight was 171 pounds.[4] Robey's toughness of body and spirit, which enabled him to play every minute of each of his team's nine games that year, was sorely tested by prejudiced opponents. At times their white fists and elbows and knees would seek to put him out of action, and often in the golden brightness of those autumn afternoons Robey had to tighten his face against the stinging sleet of racial taunts.

The black athlete's ability to overcome those vicious tactics was observed at close range by Lawrence Perry, a sports columnist and football referee. He commented that along with Robey's "immense strength" the "Herculean negro" also had

> a personality so striking that opposing players who in the early stages of a game were inclined to poke fun and sarcasm and worse at him, developed respect not only for his strength, never in any single instance misapplied, no matter what the provocation, but also for his character.
>
> The writer recalls having officiated in a football game in which he played, and observing opponents who had been particularly virulent in the first half, come to "Robey" at the end of the game to shake his hand and apologize. And well they did, for Robeson's self-control, his gentlemanly instincts and his ability as an athlete made those who had been baiting him seem like pygmies by comparison.[5]

The respectful regard he won from hostile opponents, which helped to keep him from being seriously injured, was at times achieved by means that were not less striking than Robey's personality. They were his forearms, elbows, knees, and feet that could lash out and cruelly punish an opposing player who had sought to injure him. That the retaliation was never once seen by a referee as being deliberate was a tribute to Robey's natural talents as an actor. The artfulness with which, on springing up after a tackle, Robey would "accidentally" knock the wind out of the offender or send him reeling from an elbow to the chin, was the result of long and secret practice. Also carefully rehearsed was the touching drama of his apologetic concern for the man he had bumped into. As the player sagged toward the turf, Robey would quickly catch him, lower him gently, and while cradling the dazed head in his arm, say with great feeling: "Oh! Oh! I am *so* sorry! My, my—I *do* hope I haven't *hurt* you!"

Through the years Paul would often reenact that scene for the amusement of his friends and to his own unfailing delight. His pantomime of

Paul Robeson's maternal grandfather, Charles Hicks Bustill (1816–1890), and his daughters, (left) Gertrude Emily (1855–1947) and (right) Maria Louisa (1853–1904), Paul Robeson's mother. (Unpublished photo, circa 1870, courtesy of Marian Robeson Forsythe)

Witherspoon Street Presbyterian Church in Princeton, N.J., which Rev. William D. Robeson served as pastor from 1879 to 1901. (Photographed for the author by Betty Millard)

"In loving remembrance of Sabra Robeson." Stained-glass window in
Witherspoon Street Presbyterian Church, installed by Rev. William D.
Robeson, pastor, in memory of his slaveborn mother. (Photographed for
the author by Betty Millard)

Residence at corner of Witherspoon and Green Streets in Princeton was the parsonage of Rev. William D. Robeson, pastor of the Witherspoon Street Presbyterian Church, and the birthplace of his seven children, the youngest of whom was Paul, born April 9, 1898. (Photographed for the author by Betty Millard)

St. Luke's A.M.E. Zion Church, erected in 1908 by Rev. William Robeson's congregation in Westfield, N.J. (Photo by the author)

Building erected in 1870 at Lincoln University, Pa., by Maria Louisa Bustill's uncle, Joseph C. Bustill (1822–1895). Maria Bustill met her future husband, William Robeson, while he was a student at Lincoln. (Unpublished photo, circa 1900, courtesy of Virginia Bustill Smith Rhetta)

St. Thomas A.M.E. Zion Church in Somerville, N.J., pastored by Rev. William D. Robeson from 1910 until his death in 1918. (Photo by the author)

House at 13 Green Street, Princeton, where Paul Robeson's mother, Maria Louisa, was fatally injured in a household accident on January 19, 1904. (Photographed for the author by Betty Millard)

Rutgers 1918 football team, with Robeson (front row, second from left) the college's first All-American player. (Courtesy of Special Collections and Archives, Rutgers University)

"Robeson of Rutgers," considered to be the nation's best college football player in 1917 and 1918. (Courtesy of Special Collections and Archives, Rutgers University)

The Rutgers baseball team's 5–1 victory over Princeton on June 10, 1919, was Robeson's last collegiate athletic game, his Class of 1919 having graduated earlier that day. That victory was notable for being the first for any Rutgers team in the many decades of competition with Princeton. (Courtesy of Special Collections and Archives, Rutgers University)

During his last year in Columbia Law School, Robeson played professional football with the Milwaukee Badgers. Here he is shown in an undated newspaper clipping (possibly 1921) reproduced in Eslanda Goode Robeson, Paul Robeson, Negro *(London: Victor Gollancz Ltd., 1930).*

Paul Robeson's Columbia Law School class of 1923. Robeson is in the fourth row near the end on the lefthand side. (Print courtesy of Columbia Law School Publications and Public Relations)

Robeson in 1935 at a friend's home in Pennsylvania. The sheet music shown is "Ol' Man River." (Courtesy of the photographer, Louise Dahl Wolfe)

Paul Robeson, right, in concert with Lawrence Brown, May 1947. Brown, who arranged many of the spirituals in the Robeson repertoire, occasionally added his gospel-style tenor to his partner's bass-baritone in duets of those folk songs. (UPI/Corbis–Bettmann)

Cover of a pamphlet published in 1951 by Freedom Associates in Harlem as part of an effort by Robeson supporters to win his right to travel abroad, Robeson's passport having been canceled the previous year by the State Department. (Illustration by Hugo Gellert)

Robeson in 1952, when the author became his coworker. (Courtesy of the photographer, Lotte Jacobi)

Paul Robeson, age seventy-five, with the author at Robeson's sister's home in Philadelphia, June 29, 1973. (Photo by Lily Brown)

J. Douglas Brown (1898–1986), a classmate of Robeson's at Somerville (New Jersey) High School, became dean of faculty and provost at Princeton University. (1969 photo by the author)

Looking west on Highway 64 at Robersonville, N.C., birthplace of William D. Robeson. Vernon Roberson's house is not far beyond the first house visible on the right. (October 1971 photo by the author)

Robeson's grave, Ferncliff Cemetery, Hartsdale, N.Y. (Photo by the author)

the lightning flash of his forearm or heel, the quick catch of the slumping body, and then the tender words of solicitude, was also used by him to illustrate to a black audience the value of resistance to racism: Those "accidents" had been a sure cure for malicious roughness.

Years later, Robeson told a friend, Angus Cameron, that the guiding hand of his father included advice on how he should conduct himself on the gridiron.

> Paul told me [Cameron recalled] that just before he went off to Rutgers his father said something like this: "Now son, you must remember that when you begin to play college football you, as a Negro, have to lean over backwards to be a clean player. You can't afford to break any rules. You must always play according to the rules."
>
> Then Paul went on to say: "And I can honestly tell you that never, I mean *never*, not once while I was playing college football did I use my hands illegally. And, as you know, most players always use their hands illegally if they can get away with it. I *never, never* did." Then he took on a sort of retrospective look and added, "But I'll tell you what I *did* do: I practiced breaking orange crates with my forearm."

Apart from his correctional tactics, Robey's powerful tackling could be a fearsome thing. This was acknowledged by Charley Brickley, twice All-American halfback for Harvard, who captained a Navy Transport team of former college players that suffered a 40-0 defeat by Rutgers. In that game, the *New York Times* reported, "Brickley once made five yards through the line, but he was so badly shaken up when big Robeson stopped the play that Charley tarried in the background after that."[6] And according to one of the game's officials, "Charley said one tackle by Robeson was all he cared for, and he was perfectly willing to let someone else do the honors."[7]

If it was difficult for a ball-carrier to get past the stonewall defense of Robey (his role as "defensive fullback" was essentially that of the latter-day "middle linebacker"), the task of stopping him when he carried the ball apparently was not much easier. In a game against Lehigh (won by Rutgers 39-0), Robey's running strength caused a reporter to marvel at

> how that boy can carry the ball! In the third period he leaped in the air, speared a forward pass with one hand and started for the goal line. He had not traveled five yards before he was tackled and seemed ready to fall. However, he stiffened his legs, shook off two men and started again. He was

nailed five different times on that run, but got out of every trap and crossed the goal line alone. It was one of the greatest runs I ever have seen.[8]

That driving power was observed in another game by Frederick G. Lieb, a *New York Sun* reporter who, noting that the "real Rutgers hero was the negro end, Robeson," wrote that one of his ball-carrying plays "was worth a good laugh in addition to being mighty fine football. Four Maroon tacklers were hanging on Robeson's knees as he reached into the air and drew in the football, but showing little annoyance he carried the ball for some fourteen additional yards before he was brought down."[9]

That contest, a Rutgers victory over Fordham University on October 27, 1917, was one of the two games played in New York that year that made "Robeson of Rutgers" nationally famous. The strong New York eleven, unbeaten until then, included among its stars Frank Frisch, the "Fordham Flash" who would later become a Hall of Fame baseball player and manager. But by all accounts the hero of the game was Robey. As Charles A. Taylor of the *New York Tribune* saw it: "A dark cloud upset the hopes of the Fordham eleven yesterday afternoon. Its name was Robeson, and it traveled all the way across the Jersey meadows from the banks of the Old Raritan to the Bronx. . . . The score was 28 to 0 in favor of the dark cloud."[10]

That reporter was impressed by the extraordinary, and perhaps unprecedented, game plan used by the visiting team in which "the giant negro . . . played in practically every position on the Rutgers team before the battle ended."

> With his team on the offensive, Robeson was wont to leap high in the air to grab forward passes whenever he saw that the man they were intended for was in another sector of the battlefield. . . . Robeson was supposed to play fullback on the defensive, and he did, but never did a fullback range so widely as he. If there was a gap in the line Robeson filled it. If the Rutgers ends were the least bit remiss in stopping the dashes of Erwig and Frisch, Robeson was on hand to prevent any substantial progress.

The writer who covered the game for the *New York Times,* which was then considered to be quite unfriendly to blacks, seemed to be under some constraint as he began his account of Robey's singular exploits that day. "It can hardly be said," he wrote, "that one player stood out on the Rutgers aggregation, unless it was Robeson, the giant negro at left end." But there was no inhibition as he continued:

He was a tower of strength both on the offense and defense, and it was his receiving of forward passes which shattered any hopes of glory [for] Fordham. Twice the big Rutgers negro raced down the field after receiving a perfect toss from Whitehill. The first time Robeson was not downed until he had covered thirty-five yards and placed the ball on Fordham's five-yard line. On the other occasion Robeson raced twenty-four yards before being brought to earth again close to the Fordham goal line. Each of these passes gave Rutgers a chance to score, and Rutgers did not throw away the opportunity. [The report noted that a third touchdown resulted from another Robeson carry to the five-yard line.]

However, when the anonymous *Times* reporter went on to tell about Robey's devastating blocking that tore gaping holes in the opposing line, he seemed to become almost as upset as the Fordham defenders had been: "Robeson invariably spilled two men and several times three or four were dropped to the ground, even before the play was well under way. The vicious playing of Robeson was costly to Fordham, not only in the final outcome of the game, but in players, since no less than three Fordham men were sent into the game at different times to take the place of those that had been battered and bruised by Robeson."[11]

Robey's feats in the Bronx against Fordham were followed a month later by what was judged to be an even more spectacular performance in Brooklyn. In the final game of the season, on November 24 at Ebbetts Field, Rutgers's opponent was Newport Naval Reserves. That was an all-star team of former college players, which was captained by the famous All-American of Yale, Clinton ("Cupid") Black, and considered by many to be virtually unbeatable. With a squad that included several other All-American players and a line that averaged 203 pounds, the Navy team, which had never been scored against, was touted in the pregame publicity as an all-conquering Goliath against which the Rutgers team of smaller and less experienced men would be a helpless David. But as incredibly as in the Bible story, Goliath was wiped out again; and this time the miracle was documented by duly accredited scribes.

One of them, reporting for the *Sunday Tribune,* recalled that the possibility of a Rutgers triumph had been deemed "beyond belief"; and he pointed to what he saw as the principal cause of the upset: "It was Robeson, a veritable Othello of battle, who led the dashing little Rutgers eleven to a 14-0 victory over the widely heralded Newport Naval Reserves." The reporter, Louis Lee Arms, began his story in the colorful sports-page style of his paper:

A tall, tapering Negro in a faded crimson sweater, moleskins, and a pair of worn maroon socks ranged hither and yon on a wind-whipped Flatbush field yesterday afternoon. He rode on the wings of the frigid breezes; a grim, silent and compelling figure. Whether it was Charley Barrett of old Cornell and All-American glory, or Gerrish or Gardner who tried to hurl himself through a moiling gauntlet, he was met by and stopped by this blaze of red and black.[12]

Though Robey scored one of the two Rutgers touchdowns, it was his defensive play that most impressed that reporter, who changed the *Tribune's* designation of the football star from "dark cloud" to the wondrously prophetical "Othello." He told how "Robeson, commanding Rutger's secondary, dived under and spilled [Navy's] wide, oblique angled runs, turned back her line plunges and carried the burden of the defense so splendidly that in forty-four minutes [the total playing time] these All-American backs, who are fixed luminaries in the mythology of the gridiron, made precisely two first downs."

That accomplishment moved another writer, George Daley of the *New York World,* to declare: "Paul Robeson . . . is a football genius." In his article, headlined "ROBESON TAKES A PLACE WITH ELECT OF FOOTBALL," the reporter asserted that the Rutgers star must be ranked with six other men whom he considered to be the most versatile players in the history of the sport.* To prove his case, Daley listed the "wide repertoire" shown at Ebbets Field by "this super-man of the game": "Opening up holes for his backs on line plays; providing remarkable interference for his backs on end runs; going down the field under punts; taking forward passes, in which, by the way, he handles the pigskin with almost the same sureness as a baseball; supporting the center of the line on defense; plugging up holes from one end of the line to the other; tackling here, there, and everywhere; kicking off and diagnosing." The last-named item on the list may have been the most important of Robeson's assets, according to this writer, who suggested that "The greatest perhaps of his accomplishments is accurate diagnosing. His ability to size up plays and quickly get to the point of the danger is almost uncanny. He is so

---

* With the exception of Paul Robeson, all named by Daley were later elected to the College Football Hall of Fame at Rutgers. The others were Tack Hardwick and Eddie Mahan of Harvard, Charley Barrett of Cornell, Jim Thorpe of the Carlisle Indians, Elmer Oliphant of Purdue and Army, and Ted Coy of Yale. Thorpe, whom Robeson later played against in professional football, was also elected to the Hall of Fame for professionals.

rarely at fault that he is at the center of practically every play, and therein lies his greatest value, and therein is the truest measure of his all-around ability."[13]

The subject of the black star's braininess was also commented on by Tom Thorp, a *New York Sun* writer, after he had officiated at another game where Robeson played. Stating that "as a diagnostician of plays, Robeson is in a class by himself," Thorp described the athlete's quickness of mind when playing as a defensive back: "He never budges until he sees where the ball is, and when he does he goes after the man who has it like an avenging spirit. He is never sucked in and is the fastest thinking football player I've ever seen. You simply can't fool him."[14]

Walter Camp, the dean of football experts, was among the spectators who cheered the sensational performance of the first black athlete to star at Ebbets Field.* The knowledge of his presence must have been for the players a spur much greater than any exhortation by Coach Sanford that his men do or die for dear old Rutgers, or by Cupid Black that his all-stars win another big victory for their Uncle Sam. To players and football fans alike, Walter Camp was the one-man Supreme Court of the game, an authority as unchallengeable as Noah Webster in a spelling bee. For twenty years Camp had annually selected from the rosters of the various college teams an "All-America" team composed of the players he deemed best for the eleven positions on a football squad. Though other experts made their own annual selections, Camp's choices were considered *the* All-Americans, and fans eagerly awaited his findings that were published each January in *Collier's Weekly*.

But that year was different: The nation was at war. After Walter Camp had compiled his usual roster, the *Collier's* management decided "out of deference to conditions prevailing in the country the annual selection of the All-America Team would be omitted."[15] The enforced patriotic ban (which would be lifted the second year of the war) required Camp to pick first-, second- and third-place "All-America Service Teams" from players on the various armed forces teams. However, as if to underscore the unfair procedure forced upon him by *Collier's*, Camp made a point to show his readers that the three men he picked from the Newport Naval Reserves team had been overshadowed by another, nonselected player. If he

---

*Thirty years later, in 1947, the fans at Ebbets Field, home stadium of the Brooklyn Dodgers baseball team, cheered the feats of Jackie Robinson, the first black baseball player permitted to play in the major leagues.

could not pick that man, Camp could and did name him. "The main cause of Newport's undoing," he told his readers, "lay in the giant Robeson," despite the fact that "Newport had the All-Americans Black, Callahan and Barrett, besides an assortment of other stars!"[16] And in Camp's accompanying review of the college football season, he gave more attention to Robeson than to any other player. When he appended a list of college "Stars of 1917," he placed the name of Robeson first among them all.[17]

Although there was no Camp-selected All-America college team that year, Robeson is rated as All-American for 1917 because he was the consensus choice of virtually all of the other experts for that honor.* Thus Rutgers, which in the opinion of one alumnus dishonored itself the previous year by benching Robey in deference to racial bigotry, now for the first time in its fifty-year history of football competition had the honor of a Rutgers man being named All-American.

As for Robey himself, no hero could have been more modest. His practice of that virtue, so firmly instilled by Pop's guidance and example, was now exaggerated by the social pressure not to act "uppity"—the prevailing term for any sign of arrogance in a black American. Thus there was not the faintest hint of his stardom in the review of the football season that Paul wrote at the request of a college publication.[18] In that article (his first published writing), Paul reviewed every game and warmly praised in turn each of his teammates from Captain Thug Rendell (he had a " 'never say die' spirit") down to the substitutes (they all "will bear watching") and lower still to the scrubs who couldn't make the team ("to them belongs a lot of honor" for "playing valiantly" in practice against the varsity team). But except for a single reference that named him as one of the three veterans on the team at the season's outset, All-American Robeson was benched throughout that review by Author Robeson. Not only was Robey written out of the account but his singular role was negated in Paul's ar-

---

* That consensus was verified in a definitive chronicle of the sport compiled by Col. Alexander M. Weyand, a leading football historian who was a 1915 All-American at West Point (where he was a classmate of Dwight D. Eisenhower). Weyand wrote: "Because of war conditions, Mr. Camp published no teams for 1917. Those listed for that year were prepared by the author and are based upon the consensus of various critics whose selections appeared in the annual *Guide*"; and accordingly he placed Robeson on the first team. From *The Saga of American Football* (New York: Macmillan, 1955), pp. 204, 216. Weyand's objectivity in listing Robeson as a two-time All-American (1917 and 1918) was in marked contrast to the actions of other chroniclers who omitted Robeson's name from their compilations and accounts.

ticle when he stated: "There was no individual brilliancy, but every man did his best for the common cause."*

Paul was, however, entirely sincere when he gave the main credit for the team's success to Coach Sanford ("the greatest of football coaches"). And the hero-worshiping regard he had for his mentor never dimmed in later years. Paul was writing from the heart when he said in his article that George Foster Sanford would always be remembered

> by those who have been his pupils, who have had the privilege of close as- sociation with him, who have listened to his inspiring talks, [and] have re- ceived an impetus toward higher and better things of life through obser- vance of his character . . . A wonderful coach, yes, but more, a wonderful man, an adviser, the guardian and moulder of the character of the young men under his supervision! An advocate of clean play, not only on the foot- ball field, but also in life!

Unfortunately, Rutgers had no wonder-working coach like Sanford for its basketball team; and though Robey was one of the better players on that squad he was a superstar only in some hometown and campus write- ups.† That year, playing as either forward or center on a team that won five games and lost three, Robey was Rutgers's top scorer with a season's total of thirty field goals.[19] As for his one-man vendetta against Prince- ton, he was frustrated again when the enemy's basketball team clobbered Rutgers 41 to 14 and held Robey, playing left forward, to a miserable two points. Now there would be only one more year when he might take part in a defeat of Princeton.

In his third year in college, Robey seemed to have more energy than ever before. While keeping up his high scholastic average, he now added baseball and track to his schedule of sports. On the baseball team, Robey, who played catcher, was good at that position but weak at the bat. His season's average was a lowly .143. On the track team he competed in the shot-put, javelin, and discus events; and that season he was one of Rut-

---

* Feeling perhaps that in his article Robey may have gone too far in doing the "fine thing" of abnegation expected of him at Rutgers, the editors published an introductory note that praised the black athlete's outstanding performance and observed that "he was selected by practically every football authority in the country as the season's leading player."

† Not content with asserting that "Paul Robeson is one of the best basketball players in the college," Rutgers's yearbook for 1919 (*The Scarlet Letter 1920*) also hailed him as "one of the best players of all time."

gers's two nonwinning entrants in a pentathlon competition. (In one trial he ran the 100-yard dash in eleven seconds.) Though he would later win both the javelin and discus throws in a match against Swarthmore, he was outstanding only in comparison with the relatively few others at his school who went out for track. (With a total enrollment of about 500 students, Rutgers had a scant supply of athletic manpower. And Coach Sanford must have been almost as great as Robey said he was to have led that little school to the top ranks of football.)

And then, as if playing on each season's athletic team were not enough, Robey also tried out for and won a place on the varsity debating team. Thus, on March 15, 1918, as one of the three members of that team, he took part in a debate against Trinity College on the question: "Resolved, that Universal Military Training and Service be the fixed policy at the end of the present war." Robey's side upheld the affirmative.

That March, while he was still in his teens, Paul Robeson gained national recognition in African American life as a credit to his race. He was given a place of honor in *The Crisis,* the most influential and widely read black magazine in the country, which was edited by W.E.B. Du Bois for the National Association for the Advancement of Colored People.[20] Paul and his friend and fellow black All-American, Fritz Pollard, were jointly presented as the Men of the Month in a column of that name that regularly featured the photographs and brief biographies of men and women of the "Talented Tenth" whom Dr. Du Bois saw as the potential source of black leadership. (If Paul read the March issue of that magazine the following year, when he was a senior, he may have noticed that one of the Men of the Month was an ambitious young woman named Eslanda C. Goode, who was a pathology chemist and technician in New York.[21] But whether he noticed that write-up or not, her Men of the Month clipping from *The Crisis* was destined to be pasted into Paul's scrapbook along with his own.)

Du Bois's man of the month that spring of 1918 was the man of the year at Rutgers. The college that had welcomed him with blows now hailed him as a hero:

> *All hats off to "Robie," men,*
> *All honor to his name;*
> *On the diamond, court or football field*
> *He's brought old Rutgers fame.*[22]

$\mathcal{8}$

$\mathcal{R}utgers\ 3:$
"$\mathcal{T}his\ \mathcal{N}oble\ Son$"

$\mathcal{H}$ow'm I doin', Pop?" Since his early childhood that concern, though seldom voiced, was always uppermost in Paul Robeson's mind. The approbation of his father was the end toward which all other prizes and honors were but the means. To spectators and players at the Rutgers football and baseball home games at Neilson Field or the basketball games in Ballantine Gymnasium, the elderly black preacher on the sideline may have seemed a somber figure in his black frock coat, his face an impassive mask in dark mahogany. But always for Paul the old man's presence was a cheering sight, and louder than the roars of the crowd was the silent acclaim that came to him from Pop. And at home on weekends and holidays there was always the enfolding comfort and security he found in the man who had reared him and who stood in Paul's life like the solid rock in the hymn where all other ground was sinking sand. The difference of more than fifty years in their ages had given them much of the mutually satisfying relationship of grandfather and grandson, and over the years when there were only the two of them at home there had developed between the elderly widower and the motherless boy a strong emotional bond.

Then one day Pop was gone. As quietly as he had slipped away from the North Carolina plantation when he was seventeen, William Drew Robeson, age seventy-three, departed from life on May 17, 1918, at the Somerville parsonage. The numbing shock of Pop's death after a brief illness was not lessened for Paul by the fact that Rev. Robeson had grown weak with age and was unable at times to preach on Sundays or perform other pastoral duties for St. Thomas A.M.E. Zion Church. "Reverend Robeson was a grand old man," one member of the congregation recalled, "but his ability as an orator was behind him. He had worked himself out and so naturally some of the church members wanted to get a young minister to replace him. And, of course, that hurt."[1]

The talk must have hurt young Paul much more than it did his father, who like all old preachers was wise in the ways of factionalism among the faithful and the devilment of some deacons. The hurt Paul suffered by those criticisms of his adored Pop seemed to have made a lasting impression, for in later years Paul would be unwilling to face the prospect that he himself would become a weakened old man, that people would say of him too that his abilities were behind him. In maturity he would confide to close friends that he thought that Americans, more than any other people he knew, were quick to cast aside persons who had worked themselves out; the seed of that conviction must have been planted at the time of his father's decline.

Emotionally dependent on Pop, Paul was utterly desolated by his death. Suddenly everything was turned around. All the glory was gone. The "veritable Othello of battle," who could shake off the hardest blow to body and spirit and charge through all obstacles to achieve his goals, now was plunged into utter despair. Nothing would ever be the same. Now there would be no Pop to bring the prizes to and no family home to which he and his siblings could return.

They were returning now for the funeral—the five survivors of the seven children born to William Drew and Maria Louisa Robeson. From medical school in Washington, D.C., came William Drew Robeson Jr., the oldest, who was 36; from Detroit, the banished John Bunyan Reeve Robeson, 32; from a Kentucky military camp, the Army chaplain-in-training, Rev. Benjamin Congleton Robeson, 25; from a teachers training school in West Chester, Pennsylvania, the only girl, Marian Marguerite Robeson, 23; and from nearby New Brunswick, Paul Leroy Robeson, who had just turned 20. The funeral could not be held until nine days after the death, which was the earliest that Ben could reach Somerville, and in the meantime Paul was faced with the need to fulfill his father's last expectation of him.

Pop, who had been sick in bed for the last two weeks of his life, had been unhappy at the prospect of not being present when Paul took part in his third oratorical contest at Rutgers. So the old man, whose own oratorical powers had faded, was looking forward to hearing that his favorite son had triumphed again. But he died three days before the contest, and

Paul, numbed with grief and with Pop's coffin still resting in the parson-age parlor, did not see how he could go through with it. However, others urged him not to withdraw, and Bill, who earlier had pressed Paul not to quit Rutgers after that football-tryout beating, now sought to convince his youngest brother that here was another duty he could not shirk. An account of Paul's decision and its outcome was given in one of the three Robeson items published in a Somerville weekly a few days after Rev. Robeson's death. Under the heading "Paul Robeson Wins Another Honor," a news item said in part:

> Paul Leroy Robeson, son of the late Rev. W. D. Robeson, . . . added another to his string of honors by winning the Junior Exhibition at Rutgers on Monday evening [May 20, 1918]. Because of his father's death it was feared that Paul would be unable to enter the contest, but as it was his father's wish he decided to do so. . . . Paul's subject was, "Loyalty and the American Negro," and he waxed eloquent on the part the American negro had played in past wars.[2]

Another Robeson story in the *Unionist Gazette* that week was an obit-uary that noted that Rev. Robeson "was born 73 years ago in Martin County, North Carolina," but did not mention that he had started life as a plantation slave, the son of Benjamin and Sabra, and that he had run away from his master. The account was otherwise an accurate summary of his life and achievements. A third item was a brief editorial tribute to the deceased pastor in which the white writer, untypically for that time and place, stressed William Robeson's keen concern for the rights of his people:

> The death of Rev. W. D. Robeson takes from this community one who has done a quiet but successful work among his own people for the past eight years. Mr. Robeson was a man of strong character. Educated in the south he was familiar with the characteristics of his race and was always interested in their welfare. He quickly resented any attempt to belittle them or to inter-fere with their rights. He had the temperament which had produced so many orators in the south and he held his people together in the church here with a fine discernment of their needs. He has left his impress on the col-ored race throughout the State and he will be greatly missed here.

After the funeral on Sunday, May 26, the body of William Drew Robe-son was taken to Princeton and interred beside the grave of Maria Louisa Robeson, whose tragic death had occurred fourteen years earlier.

Across the street from the cemetery stands the Witherspoon Street Presbyterian Church, "that church carved out of ebony" where William Robeson was pastor for more than twenty years and where the stained-glass window inscribed "In loving memory of Sabra Robeson" glows in tribute to his enslaved mother who had cried for sorrow and joy to see him go.

∽   ∽   ∽

Soon after the funeral, Paul's junior year at Rutgers came to an end. Along with his third oratorical prize he added yet another to the "string of honors" noted by his hometown newspaper. Because of his race he had not been admitted into any of the fraternities on the campus, but now because of his brains he was elected to membership in Phi Beta Kappa, the national honorary fraternity of scholars. That award together with his winning All-American status in football (and wide recognition as the best player in the country) was a rare combination of achievement, and Paul may have been the first football champion elected to Phi Beta Kappa.*

The two principal circumstances of Paul's life at that time were direct opposites: the nadir that was the death of his father and the zenith that was his success as an athlete and scholar. Either circumstance alone would have affected him deeply, but coming together they made a turning point in his life. Not only was Pop gone but so was Robey's zest for college, though that would not show up until the next term began.

Paul's spirits were not lifted by his dutiful attendance at the annual reunion picnic of the Bustill family, which was held on June 21 in Philadelphia, five weeks after Pop's death. Reunions of the descendants of Cyrus Bustill—Paul's mother's family—had been held each year since 1900 under the auspices of the Bustill Family Association of which Paul's aunt, Mrs. Gertrude Bustill Mossell, was an officer.[3]

Paul was able to attend the affair because that summer, owing to wartime conditions, he had not departed for work at the Rhode Island beach resort but remained in New Jersey, where he found work as a laborer in a shipyard. Three other Robeson-Bustills—Paul's brothers, Bill, Reeve, and Ben—also attended the picnic, which could not have been much fun and games in view of the lengthy formal program that took place. The program opened and closed with patriotic hymns and prayers,

---

* Paul Robeson later served as a member of the editorial board of the Phi Beta Kappa publication, *The American Scholar.*

and in between came the reading of the family's history, a necrology, and no fewer than five addresses, one of them by "Mr. Paul Roberson." (By a coincidence that typographical error in the printed program gave his surname the spelling used by his relatives in North Carolina.) The subject of Paul's speech, "Loyalty to Convictions," was chosen, he recalled later in life, because "that was the text of my father's life—loyalty to one's convictions. Unbending. Despite anything."[4]

Because of their racial admixture many of the Bustills who attended these reunions did not appear to be "colored people," as they like most African Americans then termed themselves, but were as fair-skinned and blue-eyed as any whites. Paul's sister, Marian, who somehow had not been able to come to that 1918 gathering, recalled that at another year's reunion there were present some members of the all-white branch of the Philadelphia Bustills. Marian recounted with considerable amusement a conversation she overheard between a distinguished-looking elderly white woman and a younger companion, who may have been the woman's niece. "But I can't see how these colored Bustills can be *real* Bustills, the same as we are," the younger one remarked. Then the elder explained the mystery: A long, long time ago, Samuel Bustill, the first Bustill to come to America from England, fathered a colored son, Cyrus, from whom these colored Bustills were descended. "So you see, my dear," she concluded, "they are real Bustills, though of course an entirely different branch."

As authentic as the colored Bustills were, and as authentic as was his own maternal lineage in that family sired by his great-great-grandfather Cyrus, Paul felt out of place among the assembled clan. Since childhood he had been taken by his father to the annual assemblies, and because Pop had hoped to be present at the 1918 gathering, Paul undoubtedly felt it his duty to attend. But he would never go again, and his earlier discomfiture with his maternal relatives developed into a strong displeasure. It seemed to Paul that many members of the Bustill Family Association were much too snobbish about their background and seemed to feel that the accomplishments of the notable Bustills of the past made their descendants inherently superior to ordinary blacks. They took pride in the fact that unlike most other African Americans, the Bustills had been free for generations; and the family history that was read at the reunions never revealed that the illustrious Cyrus, to whom George Washington allegedly gave a silver coin, had been born a slave. Paul, who felt no sense of shame because his own father had been a slave, did not like that his Bustill kin were ashamed of the involuntary servitude of their great-grandsire. Then too he could not help noticing that some of the fair-skinned Bustills also seemed to think that their color made them better than blacks of a darker hue. It was also evident that the colored Bustill Family Association looked with pride to a time when the Bustills had been entirely white.*

Paul's Aunt Gertrude—the dynamic "Mrs. N. F. Mossell," as she signed her numerous magazine and newspaper articles—shared the progressive outlook of her distinguished physician husband. But she antagonized young Paul by her disdainful attitude toward his relatives who were not Bustills—his father's kin who lived in Princeton. If William Robeson and his children were of the "Talented Tenth" to which Aunt Gertrude man-ifestly belonged, William's brothers, who worked as laborers, and their wives, who often worked as domestics, were plainly of the other nine-tenths that comprised the mass of ordinary African Americans. To Aunt Gertrude they were definitely not the type to be invited to a Bustill gath-ering. Paul strongly disagreed with her.

The conflict between Paul and his mother's sister on that matter was never resolved, as one of Paul's friends from childhood recalled. She was Christine Moore, who had been forbidden by her parents (her father was the richest black man in Princeton) to play with the "other Robesons" be-cause they were said to be "too common."[5] Christine Moore told how her mother had been asked to try to convince Paul to come to later Bustill re-unions. "I have written to him five or six times," her mother complained, "but he just won't answer." Paul's eventual reply, relayed through Chris-tine's mother, was this: "Well, you can tell her she can write me five or six more times, but I still won't come unless she also invites my cousins." There was no give on either side, and so neither the distinguished Paul Robeson (the famous singer and actor) nor his undistinguished Robeson cousins ever appeared at the subsequent Bustill reunions that took place over the next twenty years.[6]

Paul's alienation from the Bustill family was also demonstrated by the keen distress he felt in later years when, as frequently happened, his name appeared in various publications as Paul Bustill Robeson.[†7] Because he kept private his feelings about the Bustills, mentioning the subject only to

---

* Thus on the cover of the printed program used at the Philadelphia reunion were the coupled dates "1608–1918," to indicate the span of the family's history. Cyrus Bustill, the first black in the family, was not born until 1732.

† Named Paul Leroy by his parents, he dropped the middle name when he became an actor. Thereafter, he would admit to "Leroy," which he disliked, only when it was neces-sary to refute the erroneous—and resented—"Bustill." The principal source for the error,

close friends and even then with lowered voice, his vehemence in denying that his middle name was Bustill seemed inexplicable to others.

Christine Moore, who remembered that her father used to drive their family in his red Franklin motorcar from Princeton to Somerville to hear Rev. Robeson preach, would remain a good friend of Paul's for many years. Mrs. Christine Moore Howell (she had become the wife of Dr. Gaylord Howell, a New Brunswick physician) was noncommittal about any particular role she played in young Paul's life, but she had many happy memories of the parties she attended in Princeton, Trenton, and elsewhere where Paul was as attractive to the girls as they were to him. "Of course we were all sweet on him," she said. "You know, the strong football hero, big broad shoulders and all, and with such a polite and gentle manner, too. And then—oh my!—there was that voice when he used to sing for us!" They were always love songs, she recalled, and she often accompanied him on the parlor piano as he sang such melting ballads as "Love's Old Sweet Song," "Just A-Wearying for You," and "Because." The memory of how sweetly he sang "Because," a favorite of hers, brought another soulful "oh my!" from the gray-haired and still lovely Christine.

෨෨ ෨෨ ෨෨

When Robey returned to Rutgers that fall an even closer relationship developed between him and the football coach, who now became something of a foster-father to the young man. Coach Sanford, Paul's principal adviser and friend through college and for some years beyond, no doubt reminded his protégé that in his final year Robey had to think seriously about what he would do after graduation. Paul did not like to make long-range plans or commit himself to some future action. It was a trait that would persist and grow stronger throughout his life. But though he had always put off thinking of what he wanted to be in life, now he had to decide on something. It is likely that Sanford played an important part in Paul's decision to prepare for law school. Sanford himself was a lawyer, though not a practicing one, and he later influenced his son, George Foster Sanford Jr., to earn a law degree. Paul may also have been encouraged to decide on a law career by James Carr, Rutgers's first black graduate, who had risen in that profession to become assistant corpora-

---

which appeared in *Current Biographies* and other reference publications, was the biography of him written by his wife, Eslanda Goode Robeson, in which she stated: "They [his parents] named him Paul Bustill Robeson." As Mrs. Robeson knew his middle name was Leroy, her version reflected a snobbish partiality toward the Bustills.

tion counsel of New York City, and whom Paul had met at a banquet in that city. Paul's decision to enter law school after graduation was reflected in his choice of subjects that year, which included constitutional law, political science, and, for the fourth successive year, public speaking.

As a senior, Paul was even less of a bookworm than he had been before, and his last year was his least distinguished in scholastic achievement. In part that may have been because he no longer had Pop's pressure to get A's, and then too he may have decided that having won the Phi Beta Kappa key he no longer had to prove by superior performance that he was in fact an equal. With his change of attitude the seven A's and one B of his freshman year would diminish to two A's, four B's, one C and even a D at the end of his senior year. (The D was in economics, which he dropped after one semester.)

Robey's mentor, Coach Sanford, who stressed strength of character and physical prowess, could not have been overly concerned about his star player's scholastic decline from excellent to merely above-average. For his last year on the team, Robey had the experience of three seasons behind him and was now closer to his physical maturity. (He would be only twenty years old when he ended his football career at Rutgers—several years younger than the age generally considered to be an athlete's prime.) With the Scarlet team built around Sandy's one-man platooning of Robey at end, tackle, and fullback, the coach and his black protégé had the satisfaction of bringing Rutgers another winning year, for a total of 22 victories, 6 losses, and 3 ties during Robey's four years on the team that had at first rebuffed him.[8]

Perhaps the most impressive tribute to Robeson's gridiron prowess came at the end of that season from Walter Camp. "There never was a more serviceable end, both in attack and defense, than Robeson," the arbiter wrote in *Collier's Weekly*[9] as he named the Rutgers star to his All-America first team for 1918.*

Though he was "best in the country," Robeson was also black, and that fall he must have reflected on the ironical fact that though the world had been made "safe for democracy," racism at home still denied equality to

---

* Four of Camp's All-Americans of that year were later named to the College Football Hall of Fame, from which Paul Robeson was excluded. One of them, like Robeson a first-team choice, was Alexander, a Syracuse guard; the others, on Camp's second team, were: Henry, tackle, Washington and Jefferson; McLaren, halfback, Pittsburgh; and Flowers, fullback, Georgia Tech.

him and his people. For now his college football career came to an end on the issue with which it had begun: his right to play. The issue arose again in connection with a proposed post-season match between Rutgers and Georgia Tech, which many fans felt would determine the national college football championship. But the game was never played because the Georgia team, coached by the famous John W. Heisman, evidently believed that the concept of "white supremacy" was too precious to be tested in fair competition. A New Brunswick sports columnist had this to say: "After all the writing by the different sports writers on the plan of the game, they all overlooked the fact that no Southern team will play with a team that has a colored player on it. Georgia Tech wants to play the game without Robeson, and Sanford will not stand for it."[10] Asserting that if the Southerners played against Robey "they would be lined up against a man far superior to them," the columnist listed the black star's scholastic and athletic achievements and concluded by asking: "Is there any man on Heisman's eleven that has all these accomplishments to his credit?"

Paul, of course, was greatly pleased that this time his team had decided not to play without him, and his respect for Coach Sanford was enhanced.

At basketball too, Robey, who now played regularly at center, was a much-improved player and again was top scorer for the Scarlet team. As in football his ruggedness was often tested by opposing players who sought to put him out of action, as happened when Rutgers opened its 1918 home season with a 37-21 win over Colgate. From the outset, the New Brunswick *Daily Home News* reported, the visiting players "started by roughing Robey":

> Every time he was anywhere near the basket at least two of the opposing players were on top of him and frequently at the opening of the game he was knocked down. . . . Apparently the roughing was to no avail, for each time Robey came up with a smile, only to enter the fray with renewed pep. His playing last night was of his old-time form.[11]

That winter Robey's long-frustrated ambition to beat Princeton seemed near fruition:

> The score was 20-11 and with only ten minutes to go, things looked pretty rosy for the Rutgers team. A great big smile enveloped the face of Robey, for with Rutgers going good, how could a team, even Princeton, overcome a 9-point lead in ten minutes? Impossible. And yet it occurred. [At the very end Princeton tied the score, 20-20, and went on to win by 2 points in overtime.][12]

Robey's diehard efforts and his sad comment on the outcome were also noted in that account:

> Robeson never played a better game in his life. He was going every minute of the forty-five played. He had Grey [of Princeton], rated one of the best, if not the best center in the intercollegiate league, stopped by a big margin. Robeson outscored Grey three to one. Talking the game over yesterday, Robey said: "That was my last chance at Princeton and I sure did want to beat them. I played my hardest."

However, Fate would relent and give the unhappy young man still another "last chance." In June, Rutgers would play a baseball game against Princeton. But after that there could be no tomorrow for his hopes, because that ball game would be held on the very day he graduated.

Seemingly as inevitable as Princeton's victories over Rutgers were Paul's triumphs in the annual class oratorical contests. He celebrated his twenty-first birthday by winning the senior extemporaneous speaking contest that was held on April 23, 1919.[13] The subject was "The War's Effect on American Manhood," and Paul's remarks (of which no record exists) won him the first-place award of $30 in the seven-man contest. Another distinction that would have filled Rev. Robeson with pride was Paul's election by his classmates to Cap and Skull, the senior honor society composed of the four men deemed to best exemplify the ideals of Rutgers.[*14]

Rev. Robeson would have been disappointed, of course, that Paul, though he would graduate as an honor student, had not achieved his scholastic potential as a senior. But Pop would perhaps have decided to overlook that failure in view of the extraordinary record that his favorite son brought to Commencement Day: Phi Beta Kappa in his junior year; Cap and Skull; twice All-American in football and first Rutgers player to win that honor; lettering in four sports, with a total of thirteen letters for each of his teams; four times champion orator of his class; and finally, class valedictorian.

The class prophecy for Paul Robeson in the Commencement issue of the student magazine, *The Targum*, saw two notable achievements yet to come. The first, "He is governor of New Jersey," was strikingly optimistic

---

* Paul's own pride in that honor was recalled a decade later when he told a reporter: "The highest point in my college life and the honor I treasure most, was my election to Cap and Skull."

considering that as the Rutgers campus hero Robey had never been elected captain of any of his teams or as an officer of any of his classes, nor had he ever ranked higher than private in the khaki-uniformed Student Cadet Corps that drilled on Neilson Field during the war. (If in later years Robeson ever thought of that prediction, he might have reflected that neither he nor any other black American had ever had the chance during his lifetime to become governor of New Jersey or of any other state.)

The second forecast was: "He has dimmed the fame of Booker T. Washington and is the leader of the colored race in America." The reference to Washington reflected the general esteem still attached to the name of the black leader, who had died in 1915—the year Paul entered college.

The commencement exercises for the sixty-nine members of the Class of 1919 (about one-third of whom were in the liberal arts program with Paul) were held on June 10 in the Second Reformed Church in New Brunswick. For Paul it must have been one of the happiest days in his life. His valedictory, entitled "The New Idealism," was a great success, from the opening patriotic pronouncement—"Today we feel that America has proved true to her trust"—to the less certain-sounding but resolutely hopeful conclusion:

> And may I appeal to you who also revere their memory [the American soldiers killed in the recent war] to join with us in continuing to fight for the great principles for which they contended, until in all sections of this fair land there will be equal opportunities for all, and character shall be the standard of excellence; until men by constructive work aim toward Solon's definition of the ideal government—where any injury to the meanest citizen is an insult to the whole constitution; and until black and white shall clasp friendly hands in the consciousness of the fact that we are brethren and that God is the father of us all.[15]

But on the way to that goal, as Paul's people well know, there is always one more river to cross. Even as he delivered that speech, so filled with confidence in the future, in the back of Paul's mind there was an awareness of the urgent challenge that would come later in the day—his last chance against Princeton.

Then, in the afternoon, as he put on his catcher's chest protector, shin guards, and mask at the Neilson Field baseball diamond, Robey would have been willing to make a deal with the Devil himself and swap his Phi Beta Kappa key for a victory over the team he wanted so desperately to beat. However, there was another wonder-worker present who was on Robey's side and who toiled in partnership with him inning after inning throughout the game as—incredibly, on that last day—Rutgers beat Princeton, 5-1. No Scarlet team in years (some said never before) had won a match against the Orange and Black, but now the impossible had happened. Under the heading "Robeson Happy," the local paper observed, "It was Robeson's last game of any sort for Rutgers, and he was in there for all he was worth. He held Rule [the Rutgers pitcher] up in wonderful style and made some wonderful catches of foul flies. His line of chatter behind the bat also kept the Princeton batters worried."[16]

Contrary to some later accounts, Robey, who scored one of the Scarlet's runs, was not the hero of the game. The hero was Paul's battery mate, George "Red" Rule, who gave up only four hits and batted in the winning run. But what does it matter whose trumpet gives the loudest sound when the Walls of Jericho come tumbling down? For Paul it was a day of triumph, too long delayed but coming in the nick of time. That noted newspaper of record, the *New York Times,* duly registered Robey's happiness in a story that appeared the following Sunday. Under the headline "RUTGERS LOSES ROBESON: Giant Negro Was One of Greatest College Stars," the *Times* observed that although Robeson for the "past two years . . . has been, perhaps, the greatest player in collegiate football [he] never had the supreme pleasure of competing with a team that defeated Princeton. . . . This victory was a fitting climax to a career as a college star."[17]

Supreme pleasure is what it was. But few knew why.

The leading editorial in *The Targum* that week was devoted to the departure of Paul Robeson, who had been "this negro, unheralded and unknown" among the incoming freshmen in 1915 and had since "made a name and a record equalled by none." The sad fact was noted that his father "did not live to witness the culmination of a college career surpassed by none." In concluding, the editors wished him well and abjured Paul to be both an exemplar and a leader of his people:

Now, Paul, as you pass from our midst, take with you the respect and appreciation of us who remain behind. May your success in life be comparable to that of college days. In you the other members of your race may well find a noble example, and this leadership is your new duty.

May Rutgers never forget this noble son and may he always remember his Alma Mater.[18]

9

Rutgers 4: "To Help the Race"

*T*HERE WAS NOTHING RADICAL about Paul Robeson when he graduated from Rutgers. Indeed, he would never be more conservative. When his classmates prophesied that he would become "the leader of the colored race in America," they had more than his outstanding talents in mind. More important was the fact that Robey had what they deemed to be the right attitude on the crucial subject of race relations, and consequently his Rutgers admirers were quite sure that he would prove to be as acceptable to the dominant class of white people on a national scale as he was to that group locally. (Then, as later, it was generally considered by both races that a black leader's stature was measured by how highly he was favored by the white establishment.)

Paul himself had no ambition to become a second Booker T. Washington. For one thing, his easy-going personality was quite opposite to one who seeks political power. There was nothing in his makeup of the organization man. His goal, derived from his father's teaching, was to achieve the maximum development of his own potential, and he saw that effort as a purely personal matter, involving no judgment other than his own. Significantly, as a college sophomore he had listed as his favorite poem Rudyard Kipling's "If," a standard schoolbook preachment that equated integrity with rugged individualism: "If you can talk with crowds and keep your virtue," and so on.

But though he had no aspiration to achieve political or institutional leadership in the black community, Paul accepted the prevailing view that any African American who gained an education was duty-bound to be of service to his people. His attitude on that subject was made clear at a notable gathering held in New Brunswick a few days before he graduated. Paul, who formerly had been excluded from any banquets in that city, was now not only invited to attend but was in fact the guest of honor at a farewell dinner sponsored by the Union Civic League. Under the heading "Paul Robeson Gets Purse as Token of Esteem," the press reported that some of the town's leading citizens had wished to "show their appreciation by the presentation of a purse, and to express their regrets at the departure of one so well loved and respected."[1] Following the speeches of the various dignitaries, "Mr. Robeson in reply said he hoped his life work would be a memorial to his father's training and that his work was not for his own self but that he might help the race to a higher life."

No one present could have doubted that Paul Robeson was in fact "well loved and respected" by the leading white people of New Brunswick who arranged that send-off for the young black graduate. (The interracial banquet, unprecedented locally, was held at the YMCA because the public dining rooms would not have served the principal guest.) Nor would anyone have doubted that on his part Paul, solemn-faced and stiffly erect in his high starched collar, was earnestly looking forward to helping his people to a higher life. Thus when he was but twenty-one, and at this first public testimonial given to him, two sentiments were expressed that would become central themes in the story of Paul Robeson. One theme was how the rich white people felt about him, and the other was how he felt about the poor black people from whom he came.

For the young guest of honor, the benevolence of the better class of white people (as the upper-class group was termed by the black community) had come to be one of the certainties of his life. Since childhood the charm of Paul's personality had opened white homes and hearts to him. At Rutgers he had become the hero of that all-white campus and the protégé of the prestigious Coach Sanford, a prominent Wall Street insurance broker and friend of bankers and railroad presidents. And then on Paul's departure there was the purse and the praise from the town's elite.

But if for Robey, in the spring of 1919, interracial goodwill was a fact of his life, the situation was just the opposite for the masses of his people. As the historian John Hope Franklin would note, "The summer of 1919 . . . ushered in the greatest period of interracial strife the nation had ever witnessed."[2] Because of the bloodshed and turmoil that marked the first year after World War I, 1919 would become known in African American history as the "Red Year."* The race war, which broke out along the "color line" at home after the fighting ended on the Hindenburg Line abroad, was sparked by the rise of two opposing movements, one white, one black.

On the white side a powerful movement emerged that added the racist demand for "White Supremacy" to the chauvinistic pressure for "One Hundred Percent Americanism." The aim of that movement was to roll back whatever economic and social gains black Americans had managed to achieve during the war, when the "Uncle Sam Needs You!" posters brought large numbers of them into khaki uniforms and factory overalls. Once again, as after the end of Reconstruction, the watchword went forth: "Keep the nigger in his place." And like myriads of poisonous toadstools sprouting up overnight, the pointed white hoods of the revived Ku Klux Klan sprang up in great numbers across the land. The cause of "racial purity," which would later be symbolized in Nazi Germany by the hockenkreuz (hooked cross, or swastika), was signaled throughout America by the fiery cross of the Klan.

Now the acts of violence that during and after the war had been directed against allegedly disloyal foreigners, radicals, strikers, and pacifists (like the beaten-up and banished Rutgers freshman) became directed also—and with even greater ferocity—against the nation's black minority. The loyalty of blacks in America's wars, which in 1917 was the subject of Paul Robeson's prizewinning junior oration, did not save them in 1919, when, as Franklin writes:

> White citizens, in and out of the Klan, poured out a wrath upon the Negro population shortly after the war that could hardly be viewed as fit punishment even for a treasonable group of persons. More than 70 Negroes were lynched during the first year of the post-war period. Ten Negro soldiers, several still in their uniforms, were lynched. . . . Fourteen Negroes were burned publicly, eleven of whom were burned alive.[3]

Although most of these atrocities against black individuals occurred in Mississippi, Georgia, and other Southern states, some of the largest as-

---

* That year might also be termed the "Anti-Red Year" because of the rigorous suppression of radical dissidents by the government. In a nationwide roundup conducted in October 1919 by Attorney General A. Mitchell Palmer and his assistant, J. Edgar Hoover, more than 10,000 persons were arrested, including more than 500 noncitizens who were summarily deported. One of the latter was the noted Russian-born anarchist Emma Goldman, whom Paul Robeson came to know in London.

saults by white mobs took place in the North, where their fury was directed against entire black communities. More than a score of cities
throughout the country were the scenes of so-called race riots that began
in the summer of 1919, the bloodiest being the clash that erupted in
Chicago in July. As out of control as the Great Fire that once destroyed
that city, the conflict raged for nearly two weeks until it was finally
quelled by the militia. How fiercely Chicago's black minority fought back
against the attacking white mobs was shown by the casualty figures: Fifteen of the thirty-eight persons slain were whites, and 178 white persons
were counted among the 537 who were injured.

The black resistance in that city and elsewhere was a reflection of the
new movement that had emerged among blacks after the war. Unlike the
opposing white movement, which was arrayed in groups like the KKK,
the black movement was largely unorganized. It was the spontaneous expression of a powerful new spirit that had been stirred up among the black
masses by their wartime experiences. Just as their old-time spiritual "Did-
n't My Lord Deliver Daniel?" had added the demanding query "And why
not *every* man?" black Americans now were asking why the blessings of
democracy, said to have been preserved by victory in the war, should not
also be theirs.

Along with their large-scale migration from rural isolation to concen-
trations in industrial cities like Chicago, a militant sense of solidarity and
resistance had grown in the black communities. That militancy—a refusal
to submit passively to the attacks of their white enemies—found expression that year in a poem that would become a cultural landmark in African
American history. In that poem, "If We Must Die," Claude McKay called
upon his fellow blacks not to let themselves be slaughtered "like hogs/
Hunted and penned in an inglorious spot," but rather to return blow for
blow regardless of the odds against them: "Like men we'll face the mur-
derous, cowardly pack,/Pressed to the wall, dying, but fighting back!"*

Though it did not have a mass membership, the National Association
for the Advancement of Colored People (NAACP), led by W.E.B. Du
Bois, was the vanguard of black resistance. In June 1919, when Paul

---

* The celebrated poem, since reprinted in numerous anthologies and often recited in
the black community, first appeared in the February 1919 issue of *The Liberator,* a left-
wing magazine that succeeded *The Masses,* which had been suppressed for opposing the
war. Subsequently *The Liberator,* of which the Jamaican-born poet and novelist Claude
McKay (1891–1948) was an editor, became the *New Masses,* with which Paul Robeson
was later associated as a contributing editor. This writer was then the managing editor.

Robeson opened his valedictory address by declaring, "Today we feel that America has proved true to her trust," a national conference of the NAACP, which met later that month in Cleveland, declared that just the opposite was true. That organization, which in a later period would turn against Dr. Du Bois (he was arrested and tried as a "foreign agent") and would denounce Robeson as an "agent of the Kremlin," served notice in its conference resolution that continued black frustration might lead to "Red" involvement:

> We warn the American people that the patience of even colored people can find its limit; that with poor schools, Jim Crow methods of travel, little or no justice in courts or in things economic staring him in the face, while the colored man is called on to bear his part of the burden in taxation and in fighting the common foes of our government, we are inviting him to grasp the hands which the Bolsheviks, the I.W.W. [Industrial Workers of the World] and other kindred organizations held out to him.[4]

The NAACP then called for public agitation and pressure to secure for black Americans political, economic, and social equality and demanded that the constitutional rights granted them by the Thirteenth, Fourteenth, and Fifteenth Amendments "be recognized and enforced by the Government."

But young Robeson, after four years of education in a whiter-than-ivory tower, believed that his people's advancement would come not by militant agitation and collective struggle but by meritorious conduct. In "The New Idealism," as his graduation speech was entitled, Paul counseled that through individual effort "a way is open to welfare and happiness for all."

Paul's senior thesis,[5] submitted on May 29, 1919, just before graduation, also revealed how isolated he was from the new spirit of black militancy then beginning to arise. His thesis, based on his pre–law school studies, had as its subject the Fourteenth Amendment, enacted in 1868 to give full citizenship to the former slaves. It was a subject that lay at the center of the interracial strife that would burst into flame that summer. But in Paul's twenty-four-page paper there was no sign of awareness that the scholarly works on constitutional law cited in his bibliography had concealed the truth of racial injustice as completely as a Klansman's hood hid his face from view.

At one paragraph, where Paul extolled the Fourteenth Amendment as the greatest force assuring the nation's survival, a professorial comment was written in the margin: "Extravagant." But there was no penciled objection from that evaluator at the place where Paul, entirely unmindful of 300 years of his people's experience in America, flatly declared:

> The distinctive and characteristic feature of the American system is equality before the law. . . . As Justice Brewer says in *Magonn vs. Illinois,* "Equality in right, in protection and in burden is the thought that has run through the life of this nation and its constitutional enactments from the Declaration of Independence to the present hour." By the Fourteenth Amendment, the principle of equality before the law . . . ceased to be mere theory, or sentiment, and became incorporated into the organic law as the fundamental right of every individual.

Paul went on to cite two cases (*Strander vs. West Virginia* and *Neal vs. Delaware*) where the Supreme Court held that a "denial to citizens of the African race, because of their color, of the right to participate as jurors was a denial of equal protection of the laws." But his textbooks had provided him with no citation of the fact that for the vast majority of "citizens of the African race" such rulings of the Court were utterly worthless. Despite the large wartime migration to the North, nine out of ten black Americans still lived below the Mason-Dixon line,* where ever since the end of Reconstruction the civil rights granted by the Fourteenth and Fifteenth Amendments were, like all good things, reserved "For Whites Only."

Indeed, in that very year, 1919, a future associate justice of the Supreme Court who was then a congressman from South Carolina was pleased to acknowledge in a speech to the House of Representatives that although "the population of the Congressional district I represent is evenly divided between the races . . . the negroes of my district do not seek to participate in politics."[6] The speaker, James F. Byrnes (who later served as a United States senator, secretary of state, and governor of South Carolina) went on to urge that in the North as well "there be restriction of his [the Negro's] right to vote, because this is a white man's country, and will always remain a white man's country. So much for political equality."

---

* Because of the violence they faced in the South, blacks at that time often referred facetiously to that demarcation as the Smith & Wesson line, after the police revolver of that name.

But that is not what the books said, and Paul, agreeable by nature and dutiful by training, had no thought of challenging the authorities. The conservatism expressed in his graduation address and in his senior thesis may have been a matter of conformity as well as of conviction. (It was earlier noted that in his article reviewing the 1917 football season—the first of his three Rutgers writings that have survived—Paul, by omitting all mention of his own superior performance, had conformed to the social pressure not to appear "uppity.")

At any rate, Paul must have been satisfied with his idealistic valedictory speech, for he was pleased to give a repeat rendition of it the following month in New York. The occasion was a gathering held on July 16 at the Carlton YMCA in Brooklyn, where a program entitled "Four Negro Commencement Speakers" was presented to a black middle-class audience. Paul and three other black graduates were there to deliver the Commencement Day speeches they had made at their respective schools.* According to a black newspaper's account of the affair, its purpose was to demonstrate "the efficiency that the Race is capable of attaining" through the "broadmindedness of the leading white colleges in the East in admitting Colored students."[7]

Paul's "New Idealism" speech must have sounded rather tame, following as it did the remarks of another speaker, who "showed in a powerful manner that lynching did not consistently go with democracy and that no nation could expect to have the full fruits of peace if they permitted such conditions to prevail." Nevertheless, as the Harlem reporter noted, the "bright and particular star of the evening was Paul Le Roy Robeson . . . who was spoken of as one of the greatest students of the year by the white press, was a great athlete at school, a great singer, and a scholar of the first class."

As it happened, there was on that program another young man, who, though outshone on that occasion by the dazzling "Robeson of Rutgers," would later become one of the brightest literary stars of the "Negro Renaissance" (or Harlem Renaissance), as the black cultural upsurge of the 1920s would be called. He was Rudolph ("Bud") Fisher (the inevitable nickname derived from the name of the famous cartoonist-creator of "Mutt and Jeff"). Bud Fisher was twenty-two, a year older than Paul.

---

* The other speakers and the addresses they repeated were Rudolph Fisher, Brown University, "The Emancipation of Science"; Edwin Morgan, New York University, "Lynching and Democracy"; and Wilmer Lucas, also of NYU, "The Negro Problem and National Unity."

Like Paul, Bud was the son of a clergyman; and like Paul, Bud had been a brilliant student at a virtually all-white school—Brown University—where he had been awarded a Phi Beta Kappa key, a prize in public speaking, and the honor of being chosen as the Commencement Day speaker. That gifted young man—his greatest talent was as yet unknown—would return in the fall to Providence, Rhode Island, where his family lived, for a year's postgraduate study at Brown; and then he would go to Howard Medical School in Washington, D.C., the city where he was born.

There was warm sincerity in the congratulations the two honor graduates exchanged that evening—Paul, the future lawyer, and Bud, the physician-to-be. And later, when they kept their promises to keep in touch, they would discover that they had much more in common that their ability to prove in school the "efficiency of the Race." The two would become, in fact, "boon coons," the term then used (when no white ears were listening) for the later expression "soul buddies."

Bud Fisher would remain one of Paul's closest friends in Harlem. There in the Black Metropolis, where there were no ivory towers and The Law was a cop patrolling his beat, the textbook limitations of Rutgers's Robey would be swept away in the renaissance of black pride in uptown Harlem and the avant-garde cultural ferment in downtown Greenwich Village.

10

Harlem, Morningside Heights, and Points West

$\mathcal{P}$AUL ROBESON'S ALL-AROUND VERSATILITY during his four years at Rutgers was more than matched by the wide range of his activities over the next four years. From the summer of 1919, when he moved to New York, Paul worked his way through law school, got married, played three seasons of professional football, made his debut on Broadway as a dramatic actor, appeared there again as a singer in a hit musical show, toured England playing opposite one of that country's most famous actresses, sang numerous recitals (some for fee and some for free) at churches, schools, and community centers, served as an assistant football coach for Rutgers in New Jersey and for Lincoln University in Pennsylvania, played semi-pro basketball, tutored a Newark high school student in Latin, clerked in a Wall Street law office, and heard his wife complain in the summer of 1923 about how utterly lazy he was.

For Paul, as for anyone of African descent, moving to New York meant moving to Harlem. That Manhattan neighborhood, which had grown into a large black settlement during the previous ten years, would soon become the acknowledged metropolis of Afro-America. Not only was Harlem the most populous black urban center in the world, but as Alain Locke pointed out in 1925, it was "the first concentration in history of so many diverse elements of Negro life." The black scholar noted that Harlem has attracted the African, the West Indian, the Negro American; has brought together the Negro of the North and the Negro of the South; the man from the city and the man from the town and village; the peasant, the student, the business man, the professional man, artist, poet, musician, adventurer and worker, preacher and criminal, exploiter and social outcast. Each group has come with its own separate motives and for its own special ends, but their greatest experience has been the finding of one another.[1]

For the student and provincial Paul Robeson, the greatest experiences of his life would indeed develop from his findings in Harlem and from those who found him there.

He came as no stranger to New York's black community, for during his Rutgers years Paul had played on the basketball team of one of Harlem's most prestigious social clubs—St. Christopher. Thus he was already acquainted with most members of the social group from which would come his closest friends in the community—the young men and women who were either college students or recent graduates just entering upon careers as teachers, lawyers, and doctors. Though it was a small group (in 1920 there were only 118 black college graduates in the entire North), Paul's circle of youthful friends in Harlem would include many who later became distinguished in African American life. Among them were the writer Rudolph Fisher; the poets Gwendolyn Bennett, Countee Cullen, and Langston Hughes; the artist Aaron Douglas; the scholars E. Franklin Frazier and Charles Johnson; the political activist William L. Patterson; and the judge, Hubert T. Delany.

In one respect Paul Robeson was unique among these gifted and aspiring young people: At twenty-one he was already famous. To all of Harlem he was a hero. The respectable middle-class strivers were greatly impressed by the Phi Beta Kappa key that glinted from his watch chain, though some of them secretly may have shared the sentiments of the mass of common folk who were more dazzled by the other symbol of achievement that Paul wore—the miniature golden football of a champion. And despite the growing preachment of black pride, white opinion still counted most in measuring black worth, and Paul's prestige was especially enhanced by the fact that the white newspapers often praised him.*

---

* In later years the white press would report the exploits of numerous black athletic stars, but at that time blacks were barred from sports and so the attention given Robeson was most unusual.

But if Paul was uniquely famous, there was one circumstance he shared with all the other Harlemites: To survive he would have to "scuffle"—the community's term for any and all efforts to make ends meet. Unlike at Rutgers, Paul did not have a scholarship to attend law school in New York, and there was no one in his family who could help pay his way. Consequently, soon after graduation he found a summer job to support himself and earn some money for school enrollment in the fall. Together with Bud Fisher and Wilmer Lucas (the two had been fellow orators with Paul at the Brooklyn program of black commencement speakers), Paul got a job as a waiter on the Fall River Steamship Line, which carried passengers between New York and Boston. Because Bud was an excellent pianist (that future writer had first shown early promise as a composer), he often served as accompanist for Paul's singing as the two honor graduates earned extra money by entertaining the travelers.

By coincidence another of Paul's early accompanists at house parties and community recitals was also on that program in Brooklyn. That was May Chinn, a college student majoring in music, who followed Paul's "New Idealism" speech with several piano solos. Miss Chinn, whose cousin Chester also worked with Paul on the steamship line, became one of a group of Paul's friends who made her parents' home at 138th Street and Seventh Avenue a favorite hangout. Fifty years later and retired from her career as one of New York's pioneer black women physicians* (like Bud Fisher, May Chinn switched from music to another career), Dr. Chinn remembered the sweetness of Paul's personality. "His outstanding quality, as I recall," she said, "was that he liked people, and there was no one too low or too high for him to be relaxed with."[2] And she spoke of how warmly Paul responded to the children who gathered around him on the streets, exchanging smiles with the friendly black giant they knew to be the fabulous Robeson of Rutgers.

May Chinn saw much of Paul after he entered law school in February 1920. Paul had started his law studies at New York University in the fall of 1919, but for some reason he soon decided that he would rather attend Columbia Law School and undertook to make the change. According to M. Harold Higgins, one of Paul's Rutgers classmates who enrolled for the law course at Columbia, that school did not usually accept transferees.[3]

---

* Like black doctors throughout the country (then and for many years later), Dr. Chinn was not allowed to treat her patients when they were hospitalized, and so she began her practice as a maternity specialist, delivering her patients' babies at home.

However, Higgins, who became chairman of a bank in New Jersey, re-called taking his friend Robey to meet the dean of Columbia Law School to see what could be done to effect a transfer. The dean, Harlan F. Stone, who later served both as an associate justice and chief justice of the Supreme Court,* was impressed by Robeson's record at Rutgers and con-ditionally agreed to make him an exception to the no-transfer rule. Dean Stone's requirement—that Paul do well in his first semester's studies at NYU—was handily fulfilled, and Paul was admitted to Columbia at mid-year as a member of the Class of 1922, which had started the previous fall.

At Columbia there was no question as to whether Paul would have a dormitory roommate: He preferred to live in a furnished room in Harlem, which was only a few blocks away. That proximity, however, was only ge-ographic. To the poor black people of Harlem the prestigious, wealthy white university that overlooked their community from Morningside Heights on the west was as remote from their lives as the evening star they might glimpse in that direction. But for Paul it was a familiar expe-rience to move with ease between the two worlds of black and white, and he was self-assured both in his studies and in his relationships with his white fellow students. Columbia University was large and impersonal, with an enrollment of many thousands in its various colleges. For that reason and because he lived in Harlem where he had numerous friends, Paul did not develop many close personal ties with classmates and teach-ers as he had done at Rutgers.

Of all the faculty members Paul was most impressed by the learned Dean Stone, who taught several of his courses. (Once, many years later, when he told this writer about how greatly he as a law student had ad-mired the erudition of that future Justice, Paul went on to remark that had he himself remained in the legal profession he felt sure that his greatest satisfaction would have been in teaching constitutional law.)

Another of Paul's law school teachers who rose to prominence in the federal judiciary was Harold R. Medina, and years later their paths would cross again when Judge Medina gained national fame as he presided over the Smith Act trial of the principal officers of the Communist Party. Al-though only one of his students was a famous All-American star who stood out as a massive black presence amid all of the pale faces turned to-

---

* Named to the Court in 1925 by President Calvin Coolidge, Stone was promoted to chief justice by President Franklin D. Roosevelt in 1941. Two years earlier Roosevelt had picked for Court membership William O. Douglas, who studied under Stone at Colum-bia and attended classes there with Robeson.

ward the lecturing Medina, somehow that instructor never noticed that Paul Robeson was there. That the teacher was as totally color blind as American justice is said to be might be inferred from a letter Judge Medina would write in later years from his office as senior judge of the U.S. Court of Appeals in New York. "I have no recollection of Mr. Robeson as a student in my classes at Columbia Law School," he informed an inquirer, "and a very vague recollection of the little he had to do with the trial of the Communist leaders."[4]

While in law school and for some years thereafter Paul remained a close friend of Foster Sanford, his football coach at Rutgers. Often on weekday evenings (his weekends were for working) Paul would return to New Brunswick as a volunteer coaching assistant to Sandy. Aside from Robey's instructional abilities in the fine points of the game in which he was so versatile, Sandy must have felt that the presence of the Scarlet's first and only (until then) All-American player would be inspiring to his rookies.

And in another area, which was as ancient as football was modern, Paul's ability as a coach was also helpful to his Rutgers mentor. Sandy's son, G. Foster Sanford Jr., was having trouble learning enough high school Latin to qualify for college entrance; and so Paul would travel each week to Newark to instruct the teenager, who was thrilled to be close to the gridiron god and grateful for the expert help. That his gratitude would be lifelong was shown by a tape-recorded message sent to Robeson by the junior Sanford at a time when he was about to retire from the insurance business his father had founded. Describing himself as having been "a little insignificant brat trying to get some knowledge into my head," he told Paul he was thankful that "some of your hard work must have rubbed off," for he had done very well in his two years of Latin at Penn.[5]

That "hard work" was in fact a pleasurable activity for Paul, who throughout his life would delight in explaining to friends the various aspects of some foreign language. Milton J. Rettenberg, a classmate and friend of Robeson's at Columbia and later, was unaware of Paul's activity as a Latin tutor for Sanford's son. But years later, Rettenberg would walk into his own young son's room and see his guest, Paul Robeson (then starring in *Othello*), stretched out on the floor teaching Latin to the youngster. And the next time Robeson came he brought the boy a new and better textbook.[6]

Milton Rettenberg, who had studied music and would become a professional pianist, organized a quartet of fellow students in which Paul sang bass. Though the baritone, Billy Moore, had played football for Paul's special enemy, Princeton, they sang harmoniously together (along with the two Low brothers from Amherst) at various school functions. Another extracurricular activity of their class was basketball. As graduate students those in law school were not eligible for any of Columbia's varsity teams, but because there were some outstanding basketball players in his class, Rettenberg—not himself a player—helped form a team to play for pay on weekends against other semipro teams in the New York area. Paul and another former basketball star from Rutgers named Taliafero joined the squad.

The team members' earnings—a share of the gate receipts—were not memorable, but on one occasion there was for Rettenberg a never-to-be-forgotten experience involving the black member of his team. The incident, "which gave us a great deal of hurt inside," he recalled, occurred in connection with a game against a factory team in nearby Yonkers. The opposing team refused to permit Paul to use the locker room, and he had to change clothes in the toilet. "That was one of the experiences," Rettenberg said, "that I explained to the FBI at a time [in the 1950s] when they were interested in getting a picture of Paul's background after he had indulged in some of these pro-Red enterprises. I said maybe I could not excuse Paul, but I could always explain him." And in addition to the Yonkers incident, Rettenberg recounted to the government agent stories he had heard his black classmate tell of racist taunts and illegal physical punishment suffered in college football games.

As for Paul himself the experience of being barred from that dressing room could not have been especially traumatic, because for him as for all other African Americans racial discrimination was the rule and not the exception. Had the exceptional occurred—had his white teammates refused to play unless he was given equal treatment—the incident would surely have been unforgettable for Paul. But as it was, he seemed to have forgotten about basketball whenever he recalled his years at Columbia.

Whereas his playing of semipro basketball was then and later of little significance to Paul, there was another off-campus sport that meant a lot to him. That was professional football, which largely paid his way through law school. Paul rarely referred to that activity when he reminisced about his days as a football player. For one thing he had won his laurels as a college player. Then too in that period there was a certain social stigma attached to professional athletics. The two traditionally popular professional sports—boxing and baseball—had fallen in public esteem. Jack Dempsey, who became heavyweight champion in 1919, was widely scorned as a "slacker" for not enlisting for military service during the war. And baseball, long acclaimed as the "national pastime," was under a cloud because of the so-called Black Sox scandal of 1919, when eight players for the Chicago White Sox conspired with gamblers and caused their favored team to lose the World Series to Cincinnati. Farthest down in popularity was professional football. Then in its infancy, pro football was considered disreputable in comparison with the college game, which had been nurtured in such upper-class schools as Harvard, Yale, and Princeton. The only honorable way to "die for dear old Rutgers" was as an amateur; to play for pay was to sink to the level of manual labor.

In deference to that Ivy League attitude, which he himself could not possibly share, Paul was reticent from the outset about the part he played as one of the pioneer players in pro football. According to Harold Higgins, Paul's classmate at both Rutgers and Columbia, it began to be noticed in the fall of 1920 that the black student was habitually absent from school on Friday afternoons and also missed the classes held on Saturday mornings. "Then we discovered the reason," Higgins recalled. "Every weekend Robey was away playing football for a team in Ohio." In that connection Milton Rettenberg was pleased to remember that his lecture notes and those of another New Yorker, Philip Adler (Class of '21), were used by Paul to catch up on the topics he had missed. "And he did very well, too," said Rettenberg, "for he was an unbelievable intellect."

Paul got into pro football through Fritz Pollard, the black former All-American at Brown against whom Paul had played while at Rutgers. When Paul entered law school Fritz was head football coach at Lincoln University, the alma mater of Paul's father and his brother, Bill. At Fritz's invitation Paul accepted the part-time post of assistant coach at that black men's college where there was little pay but much pleasure for him on weekends. In addition to the rollicking good fellowship of Pollard and the Lincoln undergraduates, Paul enjoyed the parties that invariably followed the workouts and games. And now as an adopted Lincoln man Paul had the opportunity (denied him at Rutgers) of joining a college fraternity. He enrolled in the local chapter of Alpha Phi Alpha, one of the most prestigious of black organizations.

To augment his own meager earnings, Coach Pollard began to accept offers to play in professional football matches; and somewhat later Paul decided to join his chum in playing for one of the teams in Ohio, where the pro game had developed around such famous early barnstorming teams as the Canton Bulldogs.

That year, 1920, happened to be Year One in the history of organized pro football, with the formation on September 17 in Canton of the American Professional Football Association (which two years later became the

National Football League). And, strangely, the fledgling professional sport was quite un-American in one respect in comparison with the long-established "national pastime" of professional baseball: Blacks were not barred. Consequently the two black All-American stars, Pollard and Robeson, were welcomed as members of the Akron Pros, one of the eleven teams in the league.* Also on Akron's roster was Bob "Nasty" Nash, a tackle who had been the star of the 1915 Rutgers team that Robey had made the hard way; and there were several other former teammates who joined pro teams, among them Budge Garrett and Thug Rendell.

Fritz Pollard would always insist that their team won the league championship that year, a not unreasonable claim since Akron won all of its games—ten straight shutouts, according to Pollard. However, the loosely managed league, which kept few records, arranged a postseason championship play-off in which Buffalo defeated Canton and then played a scoreless tie with Akron, leaving the title officially unresolved. Thus, though it had no significance for him, the twice-All-America "Robeson of Rutgers" was one of the stars of the first season of organized pro football and a participant in the first championship play-off.

After playing a second year for Akron in 1921 (the team finished third that season with seven wins, two losses, and one tie), Robeson and Pollard joined the Milwaukee Badgers for the 1922 season—Paul's last year in law school.

Pro games were played on Sunday, but for a player to get paid (from $50 to $200 and more per game, depending on his popularity) he had to be present for practice the day before. That required Paul to take the train from New York to Philadelphia, and then, joined by Fritz, travel through the night by railroad coach to any one of a dozen cities—from Buffalo in the East to Chicago in the West—where their next game was scheduled. And then, after Sunday's bruising encounter, Paul would have another all-night coach ride back to New York and Morningside Heights for Monday's less-strenuous grappling with such subjects as Property II: Sales, Trusts, and Wills.

---

* The other teams that were assessed the $100 franchise fee to join were the Canton Bulldogs, Chicago Cardinals, Cleveland Indians, Dayton Triangles, Decatur Staleys, Hammond Pros, Massillon Tigers, Muncie Tigers, Rochester Jeffersons, and Rock Island Independents. Two teams (Massillon and Muncie) soon folded, but four more joined during the season—the Buffalo All-Americans, Chicago Tigers, Columbus Panhandlers, and Detroit Heralds.

Though he seldom talked about his pro football days and kept no records of his three seasons of play, Paul was moved in his final season to reopen his college scrapbook and paste in a few clippings that dealt with the athletic employment that enabled him to become a lawyer. One was a Milwaukee newspaper item that under the caption "Star with Local Pros" showed photographs of Robeson and Pollard and highly praised the playing of the two in a story that began with a commonplace racist witticism: "They may be dark but they are bright when engaged in combat." Another clipping, reporting the Milwaukee Badgers' 20-0 victory in their opening game, noted that "Fritz Pollard, former All-American halfback at Brown, was the chief ground-gainer for the winners"; and that "Another big star who drew rounds of applause from the excellent crowd of 1,000 was Robeson, giant colored end. . . . The visiting backs found it impossible to get around him, and on offense he picked forward passes out of the air from any position."[8]

One game at Milwaukee's Athletic Park on November 19, 1922, must have been highly pleasing to Paul, as a much greater turnout of 8,000 fans saw him score both of his team's touchdowns in their 13-0 victory over the Marion (Ohio) Oorang Indians. Leading the all-Indian team, whose players had names like Big Bear, Lone Wolf, Long Time Sleep, Chief Downwind, and Eagle Feather, was the legendary Jim Thorpe. A member of the Sac tribe of Oklahoma, Thorpe was then and later considered to have been the greatest all-around athlete in American history, having been a peerless football player with the Carlisle Indians, the winner of both the decathlon and pentathlon events at the 1912 Olympic Games, and later a major league baseball player for the New York Giants. In that game against Milwaukee, Thorpe, who was thirty-three and past his prime, nevertheless played the entire game and thrilled the fans by the flashes of brilliance he displayed in kicking, passing, and carrying the ball. There were cheers, too, for another all-time great on the Oorang team, "Indian Joe" Guyon, who like Thorpe was later installed in the Pro Football Hall of Fame at Canton, Ohio.

The star attraction on the Milwaukee team was Alvin "Bo" McMillin, the famed All-American quarterback from Centre College, who joined the Badgers for that game.* As one sports writer noted, the big crowd had

---

* Of the four All-Americans playing for Milwaukee that day, three—McMillin, Alexander (guard, Syracuse), and Pollard—were later named to the College Football Hall of Fame. The fourth, Paul Robeson, was denied that recognition.

been drawn to the game "by the opportunity to see two of the greatest
backs of all time [Thorpe and McMillin] oppose each other."⁹ But the reporter pointed out that "No whit less conspicuous than these two was
Robeson, Milwaukee's giant end. He made both Milwaukee's touchdowns, was in the thick of every play and stood out head and shoulders
over every other lineman in the game."

When Eagle Feather, fullback for the Indians, fumbled on their own
13-yard line, "a wild scramble occurred for the ball, which Robeson
scooped up" and carried over the goal line. And "the second score came as
the result of a pass, Purdy to Robeson, which the big end grabbed among
a flock of Indian backs, running 20 yards to a touchdown."

How fiercely the Indian team fought to win was shown by the fact that
three of the Badger players were carried off the field with broken bones.
The Milwaukee fullback, Garrett, who himself was of Indian parentage,
had a broken ankle; Bigbee, the right halfback who was white, suffered a
fractured shoulder blade; and Pollard, the black left halfback, had three
cracked ribs. That Paul Robeson, who as usual played the entire game,
was not on that multiracial casualty list may have been due to the respect
he evoked from opposing players. Pearl Fisher, sister of Paul's chum, Bud
Fisher, recalled that young Paul once told a group of his Harlem friends:
"It wasn't that I was so good at playing football. I just scared the opposing player to death with my *bad* look, and that other guy would think:
'That big nigger is going to kill me!'—and I'd just go right on through."¹⁰

Fritz Pollard would continue for several years more in pro football, becoming the first black coach in the National Football League (for Ham-
mond, Indiana, 1923–1925). But as he recalled, "Paul had no interest in
playing except to earn money to get through Columbia. He was set on becoming a lawyer."

Pollard was wrong about that. Robeson's undistinguished academic
record at Columbia was a clear indication that he had no real ambition to
be a lawyer. Thirty years later he told this writer that aside from his interest in legal theory, the practice of law would not have suited his personality. "My brother Bill aimed to be a physician, and he finally reached
that goal. My brother Ben knew from the outset that he wanted to be a
minister like my father. Marian wanted to be a teacher like my mother.
But me, I really didn't know what I wanted to be and I had no idea what
my future would be."

As it happened his future came to him while he was still in law school.
There was a young woman who persuaded him to take part in an amateur

play in Harlem, his first unintended step toward a thirty-five-year career as an actor. There was a young black musician from Florida whom he chanced to meet in London who moved him to a parallel career as a concert singer. And then there was a determined young woman who decided to marry him and hitch her wagon to a rising star.

$\mathcal{O}$ 11 $\mathcal{O}$

"On My Journey Now"

$\mathcal{I}$T WAS LATE IN THE FALL OF 1921, in Paul's second year as a law student and part-time football pro. "We were on our way to Buffalo," Fritz Pollard recalled,

> and Paul and I were talking about this and that when all of a sudden he turned to me and asked: "How well do you know Essie?" I said, "Well, I know her well enough to know she's not going to marry any man unless he is a big shot. Her family is that way." But then he didn't say another word— you know how close-mouthed Paul is. So we went up and played Buffalo and they beat us seven to nothing. And then coming back on the train we were yackety-yacking about losing that game when right out of the clear blue sky he said, "Well, I married Essie—last August."[1]

Though that startling revelation came several months after the event, Pollard was one of the first to hear about the secret wedding of Paul Robeson and Eslanda Goode. Their marriage would somehow endure until Essie died forty-four years later.

$\mathcal{O}$ $\mathcal{O}$ $\mathcal{O}$

If ever there was a uniting of opposites it was the marriage of Paul Robeson and Eslanda Cardozo Goode, known throughout her life as Essie. The marked differences in personality, habits, traits, and interests that existed between the two—differences that Essie would itemize, sometimes tolerantly and sometimes bitterly—was the result of their quite opposite upbringings. Paul, whose mother died when he was six, was raised by his slaveborn father, a scholarly, easygoing, warmhearted, and generous man whose quiet sense of pride was based upon his successful climb from fieldhand to clergyman. Essie, whose father died when she was four, was raised by her mother—a strong-willed, near-white woman who was ambitious, inflexible, and noted for an aristocratic manner that expressed this firm conviction: Because of its color and class lineage her family was greatly superior not only to other blacks but to most whites as well.

Essie's mother's maiden name was Eslanda Cardozo, and from the outset when she named her only daughter Eslanda Cardozo it seemed clear that the mother was determined to raise her third and last-born child in her own image. Unlike Paul Robeson, who as we have seen, frequently talked about his father, Essie never made public reference to the widow who raised her. On the many occasions when she mentioned her family background, Essie talked only of her mother's father, and in so doing she followed the pattern set by the elder Eslanda, who was always quick to let people know whose daughter she was. (This writer once remarked to Paul, "To hear Essie talk, one gets the idea that she had only one ancestor, her grandfather. Why is that?" Paul glanced around in a conspiratorial manner and whispered in a tone of exaggerated awe: "Don't you know? That grandfather was a *Cardozo!*")

The Grandfather Cardozo so frequently mentioned by Essie in speeches and articles was Francis Lewis Cardozo, a notable figure in African American history who during the Reconstruction period served as secretary of state (1868–1872) and state treasurer (1872–1876) in his native state of South Carolina. Francis Cardozo, who was born in Charleston in 1837, was the son of Jacob Nuñez Cardozo, of an upper-class family of Spanish-Jews,* and his mistress, a black woman of mixed race.

Essie was living in Harlem and working as a laboratory technician at nearby Presbyterian Hospital when she met Paul Robeson soon after his enrollment in Columbia Law School. Her ambition, she would recall, was to become a physician, but after meeting Paul, Essie changed her mind as to what she wanted to be. She decided to become Mrs. Paul Robeson. A big obstacle to that goal was Geraldine Neale, whom Paul planned to marry after law school. Another problem was the fact that many of the prettiest girls in Harlem also had eyes on Paul. Like a football quarterback at the center of a huddle, Paul was then, as later, surrounded at public appearances and social gatherings by female admirers.

---

* A scion of a different branch of that family was Benjamin Nathan Cardozo, an associate justice of the U. S. Supreme Court, who served from 1932 until his death in 1938.

However, these obstacles could not faze a daughter of Madame Cardozo, as her mother called herself. Paul's projected marriage was three long years away, and Gerry was in Washington—200 miles distant from New York where Essie and her quarry lived.

Proximity and persistence won the day, and Essie got her man. Without telling any of Paul's friends and family, who would have been very unhappy that he had not married Gerry, Paul and Essie were secretly wed by a justice of the peace in suburban Port Chester, New York, on August 17, 1921. The newlyweds decided to keep their union a secret and would not live together until after Paul finished law school and could earn a living.

Another young Harlem woman had eagerly pursued Paul before Essie landed him, but Dora Cole Norman, a married woman, had a different goal in mind. In 1920, a year before the Robesons' marriage, Mrs. Norman persuaded the reluctant but good-hearted law student to take part in a one-act play presented at the Harlem branch of the Young Women's Christian Association by the Colored Players Guild. Rev. Robeson would have been pleased to see his son, whom he had coached in parlor recitations, play the role of Simon, a black man said to have helped Christ carry the cross to the Crucifixion.* Whatever was to be his future, Paul was certain that he did not want to become an actor, and he was not at all impressed by the fact that his performance had pleased some theater people from downtown who witnessed the show. Among those who introduced themselves to compliment Paul were two rising stars of the American theater—Robert Edmond Jones and Kenneth Macgowan, both members of the Provincetown Players, an avant-garde group seeking to develop a noncommercial, humanistic theater. These scouts from Greenwich Village were harbingers of Robeson's future on the stage. It was the pull of that group combined with the pushing of his wife that eventually moved him to become a professional actor.

Two years later, in the spring of 1922, Dora Cole Norman had no problem getting Paul onto a stage again. With the end of the pro-football season, he needed the money he could earn by appearing in a Broadway production in which she and other members of the Colored Actors Guild would take part. *Taboo,* a play about blacks, was the first work of a remarkably ungifted young white woman. Somehow the drama managed to

---

* *Simon, the Cyrenian,* by Ridgely Torrence, was part of a New York production in 1917 titled *Three Plays for a Negro Theatre.* That it was generally accepted that white writers such as Torrence would be the playwrights for a prospective black theater was an indication of the cultural lag that preceded the Negro Renaissance of the 1920s.

survive four matinee performances before its final merciful curtain. ("What was it all about?" Paul once said to this writer. "I think I've got the script somewhere. Maybe you can read it and tell *me*.") It was about life on a Louisiana plantation, of which the playwright knew nothing, and there was a dream flashback to Africa, of which the writer knew even less.

A reviewer who found *Taboo* to be "obscure and diffuse" must have surprised Paul by reporting that he "dominates the play as the wandering Jim." His "rich, mellow voice" was also praised."[2] Paul recalled being somewhat alarmed one day at school when Dean Harlan Stone stopped him to ask, "Robeson, *what* are you doing?" But Paul was relieved when the future chief justice, who was carrying a newspaper, went on to say, "I've been reading some nice things about you. They say you're a very fine actor."[3]

Happily for Paul's later audiences, that wretched vehicle moved him on his way toward stardom as actor and concert singer. The amateur author of *Taboo*, Mary Hoyt Wiborg, who was as rich in money as she was poor in talent, soon promoted a revival of her play in Great Britain. The importation of the drama, renamed *Voodoo*, was financed by the noted English actress Mrs. Patrick Campbell, who would play the leading role, a dual part as Southern plantation owner and an African voodoo queen. Mrs. Pat—star, director, and producer—also rewrote sections of the impossible script and undertook a month-long tour of the provinces, hoping that a major promoter would sponsor a London production. But the play flopped, and to the baffled reviewers the main attraction was Paul's numerous songs in the part of Jim, a wandering minstrel. ("The audiences loved 'Old Black Joe,'" Paul recalled, "thinking it was a Negro spiritual.")

Because his pay was minimal during the tryout period of the play (which never went beyond that point), Paul found lodging not in hotels but in the modest homes of English and Scottish persons who took in roomers; and the kindliness with which he and the other black actors were treated by their hosts made a lasting impression on him. The warm civility of the families with whom he stayed made young Robeson feel more at home in their country than he would ever feel as a touring performer in his own homeland. That early favorable impression would grow through the years and bring him back again and again to England, Scotland, and Wales, and to associations that would revolutionize his thinking and profoundly affect his actions as artist and man.

A turning point in Paul's life came in London, where he spent a few days after *Voodoo* gave up the ghost. That was his chance encounter with Lawrence Brown, one of the events that would convince Paul that some fateful destiny was working on his behalf. Brown was a twenty-eight-year-old pianist who had come to England two years earlier to study composition at Trinity College and soon thereafter became accompanist for the celebrated black concert singer Roland Hayes. By the time Paul met him, Brown had already acquired the debonair mannerisms of a London-man-about-town that he would keep throughout his life. But contrasting with that bon vivant style (he would become known as one of the best-dressed men in London) was Brown's underlying seriousness that was reflected in his large collection of books on history and social criticism. Robeson, who was not yet the bookish person he would become, was impressed by Brown's cultivated reading. And more significantly, Paul, who would later develop a passionate concern for African American culture and its African roots, was deeply impressed by Brown's creative interest in his people's folk music.

Born on August 29, 1893, in Jacksonville, Florida, Brown, like Robeson, was the son of a former slave, Clark Brown. And as it happened with Paul, Larry's mother died when he was very young. A stepmother, Cenia, saved every penny she could to pay for the boy's piano lessons at fifty cents per session, believing that the lad could become a fine musician. Four years after high school, Larry left home to go to Boston, determined to fulfill his stepmother's hopes.

> Why Boston, and not Philadelphia or New York? Well, old chap, I'll tell you [Brown recalled]. I heard that Boston was the Athens of America, and that anyone who wanted to be a serious musician had to study in Boston. And there was something else. You see, as a youngster I was filled with race pride—I've been like that all my life—and I was set on growing up to be a credit to our race. For instance, all the bad things they said about Negroes—I was determined to be just the opposite. I decided I was never going to be uncouth or boisterous, and never be lazy or dirty or careless, and never commit rape or come to work late.[4]

Though Boston was the Athens of America, its temples of learning were not open to that would-be serious musician, and for four years Larry worked as an elevator operator in a residential hotel. The winsome personality of the handsome young man won the goodwill of the well-to-do residents; and when his ambition to study music became known a collection was made by the tenants to provide Larry with the $8 weekly subsistence he required for a two-year course of full-time music study. Then in 1920, a woman philanthropist gave him the $800 he needed to continue his studies in London.

Thus when Paul met him two summers later, Brown had already published the first of his now-classic arrangements of the spirituals (the song was "Steal Away") and was settled in his profession. Except for concert tours with Roland Hayes, with whom he was accompanist for five years, Larry had no intention of ever returning to live in his homeland. Consequently, when he gave his "Cheerio, old chap" farewell to the departing young law student and said he would be sure to look Paul up if he ever got back to the States, Brown was thinking to himself: Which will be never if I can help it!

As for Paul, he could not wait to get back to Essie, the separation having made his heart grow fonder. Then too he had to begin his third and final year in law school while supporting his wife, with whom he was now openly living, by playing a last season of professional football that would end that November in Chicago. When Robeson entered Columbia in February 1920, he was counted as a member of the Class of 1922, which was then in the middle of its first year, and he was included in the official photograph of that class. But because he graduated a half year after the others, the university would list him as one of the 220-member Class of 1923.

Paul never took the bar examination, and his brief experience as a law clerk that summer in a Wall Street firm headed by a Rutgers alumnus added to his lack of interest in a law career. The racial discourtesies expressed by the other employees would have been overcome if Paul had the ambition to be a lawyer that he had shown in overcoming not mere verbal slights but physical abuse to become a college football player.

Now enter the Provincetown Players. Paul was wanted for the leading role in a new play by Eugene O'Neill, one of the three directors of that Greenwich Village group. With his appearance the following year in *All God's Chillun* and his subsequent starring role in *The Emperor Jones,* Robeson had now become a professional actor; he had embarked on a career that would reach theatrical glory twenty years later in his *Othello,* whose 296-day run set an unbroken record for a Shakespearean play on Broadway.[5]

Happily for Paul as an actor whose race barred him from a wide variety of roles, his richly melodious speaking voice could also be expressed in song. Lawrence Brown, who broke his vow never to return to a racist America, soon joined up with Paul, whose career as a concert singer began simultaneously with that of actor. The noted tenor Roland Hayes had included a few Negro spirituals in his repertoire of mainly European classic songs, a practice later followed by the celebrated contralto Marian Anderson. But Robeson and Brown decided on something new: For the first five years of their concertizing, all of their songs would be African American, both the slave-created spirituals and the secular songs of contemporary black composers.

As Paul would recall:

> Early in my professional career I had the great good fortune to become associated with Lawrence Brown, an extraordinarily gifted Negro composer and arranger, and over the years this association grew into a successful partnership and personal friendship. It was this musician who clarified my instinctive feeling that the simple, beautiful songs of my childhood, heard every Sunday in church and every day at home and in the community—the great poetic song-sermons of the Negro preacher and the congregation, the work songs and blues of my father's folk from the plantations of North Carolina—should become important concert material. Lawrence Brown . . . was firm in his conviction that our music—Negro music of African and American derivation—was in the tradition of the world's great folk music.[6]

Having demonstrated that truth to concert audiences at home and abroad and in many phonograph recordings, Robeson and Brown, who were by no means cultural nationalists, went on to enlarge their repertoire to include songs of many nations, some of which became standard features of their programs. Combining an impeccable rendition of the native tongue with English translations, Robeson presented songs in Spanish, Czech, French, German, Russian, Yiddish, Hebrew, Polish, Chinese, Welsh, Gaelic, and Norwegian. There were also American folk ballads and labor songs. In the 1940s Robeson's recording of "Ballad for Americans" made him a spokesman for the popular left-wing concept that all ethnic, religious, and occupational divisions of the American people should unite for the common good.

In his art, Robeson understood the relationship of a keen concern for one's own people and a universalist humanism. The Irish poet William Butler Yeats expressed that thought when he wrote that in its literature a nation should see "the sacred drama of its own history; every spectator finding self and neighbor there, *finding all the world there* as we find the sun in the bright spot under the burning glass" (emphasis added). Though Robeson was often termed a citizen of the world, his life was rooted in the liberation struggles of his own people and their best representatives— men and women like Nat Turner, Frederick Douglass, Harriet Tubman, Sojourner Truth; the many unsung black abolitionists, such as those in the family of Maria Louisa Bustill; and the countless thousands of resisting slaves, such as William Drew Robeson.

At the outset of his career as an actor and singer, Paul felt certain that he could best serve the advancement of his people through his individual efforts as an artist rather than by taking part in any militant movements. In 1925, at age 28, he wrote that "one of the great measures of a people is its culture, its artistic stature," and he went on to say, "Today Roland Hayes [the aforementioned noted black tenor] is infinitely more of an asset than many who 'talk' at great length. Thousands of people hear him, see him, are moved by him, and are brought to a clearer understanding of human values. If I can do something of a like nature, I shall be happy."[7]

Robeson's highly developed sense of self-esteem served as a protective shield in his encounters with the overt racism that was then customary, such as being made to use the freight elevator when visiting white friends. One of those early friends, Walter Abel, a director and actor at the Provincetown Playhouse and later a Hollywood movie star, would recall that prior to any visit by Paul to his apartment on West 71 Street, Abel would advise the doorman that "the great artist Paul Robeson is coming, and there should be no nonsense." Recalling that Paul and Essie were not permitted to eat in downtown restaurants, Abel said, with an actor's dramatic emphasis, "Paul never gave a damn. That spirit of his was *so* big, there was no militancy in him *whatsoever*—nothing but *dignity* and *pride in himself* and his background. This was the wonderful thing. This was a great *person!*"[8]

A few years later, when Abel was in a play in London where Robeson was appearing in *Show Boat,* the Provincetowner found that his black friend was treated infinitely better in England than in his homeland. "So here was Paul, the *toast of London*—wow!" Abel told of a memorable occasion when he and his wife were guests of Paul and Essie at their home on Hampstead Heath, "next to Ramsay MacDonald."* After a sumptuous lunch served with champagne, the Robesons' chauffeured Daimler took the actors to their respective theaters, the shades of the limousine being drawn to avoid being surrounded by crowds of Robeson admirers.

Paradoxically, it was in Britain, home to his meteoric rise to top stardom on stage, screen, and concert hall, that Paul came to believe that through artistry alone he could not achieve his twin goals of self-fulfillment and

---

* James Ramsay MacDonald (1866–1937) became the Labour Party's first prime minister in 1924.

service to his people. The first phase of that transformation began with what he called his discovery of Africa in England and his subsequent quest to learn the history and culture of the scorned "Dark Continent," the ancestral homeland of his people. London was uniquely qualified as the starting point for that cultural odyssey because of the presence there of numerous African students and laborers as well as schools where he could study various African languages. Among his African friends and acquaintances were men like Jomo Kenyatta, who dreamed of the emancipation of his country from colonial rule.

In the heart of the British Empire, then at its zenith, Robeson became a militant anti-imperialist, and he soon broadened that concern to include not only Africa but other colonial countries like India, whose cause he championed in association with revolutionaries like Jawaharlal Nehru, the future prime minister of India, who was a Robeson friend in London.

From being a militant anti-imperialist, he moved on to become an anti-capitalist as well. Visits to the Soviet Union convinced him that the advancements being made there by the nonwhite peoples who had been subjugated in the Czarist Empire showed that national emancipation could best be served by the development of a socialist society.

As a man of the Left in Britain, Robeson developed strong ties with both leaders and rank-and-file members of the labor movement, among them Communists who became lifetime friends. Then too there were close attachments to various left-wing intellectuals who were an important element in the arts, sciences, and professions of that country. With his characteristic ease in moving between groups of disparate class and color, Robeson developed friendships among African dockworkers and Oxford dons.

It was as a participant in the antifascist movement of the 1930s that he began to give priority to his political activism. As an Afro-American, he was impressed by the virulent racism of the Nazis, which he saw firsthand during the early months of the Hitler regime in Germany. "Really, it was like seeing the Ku Klux Klan in power," he would tell this writer. "Brown shirts instead of white sheets, but the same idea." It was that sense of the menace of rule by white supremacists, the Master Race ideology of Hitlerism, that brought Robeson to a major turning point in his life.

That defining moment occurred during the Spanish Civil War when he visited and sang for the international volunteers who were fighting against the fascist counterrevolution backed by Hitler and Mussolini. Strangely, it was his meeting there with men from the United States who were considered "un-American" at home that convinced Robeson that he

T H E   Y O U N G   P A U L   R O B E S O N

should return from his long stay abroad. "A new, warm feeling for my homeland grew within me," he recalled, "as I met the men of the Abraham Lincoln Brigade—the thousands of brave young Americans who had crossed the sea to fight and die" in the struggle against fascism.[9] He was deeply moved to see that not only were black Americans serving in that integrated brigade, but for the first time in U.S. military history some of his people were in command positions.

When he returned to the United States the following year, Robeson had resolved to continue his activity as an antifascist and to simultaneously work for equal rights for his people at home and for colonial liberation abroad. His organizational center would be the Council on African Affairs, which he served as national chairman until it was banned for "un-American" activity in the so-called McCarthy era.

However, long before Senator Joseph McCarthy achieved his brief stardom in the media as an anti-Communist crusader, Paul Robeson was listed as a danger to national security by the Federal Bureau of Investigation, headed by J. Edgar Hoover, a white supremacist who saw all antifascists as being subversive candidates for "potential detention." One of the first entries in the lengthy dossier compiled by the FBI concerning Robeson was made in reference to a speech he made in Boston on November 14, 1943. On an off-day from his starring Broadway role as Othello, Robeson appeared in the Massachusetts capital to speak at a Symphony Hall rally in support of the anti-Hitler war effort and to denounce certain fascist-like events that had occurred in the Boston area.

(During the previous month there had been several anti-Semitic attacks against Jewish institutions and stores in nearby Dorchester and Roxbury, involving window smashing and painting of swastikas. Followers of the notorious Charles E. Coughlin were reported to be the perpetrators. Before the war, Father Coughlin, a Michigan Catholic priest with a huge nationwide radio audience, had denounced Jews as international bankers who dominated Wall Street and as bloodsucking leeches destroying the American way of life.)

In his remarks, Robeson said the racist outrages were "terrifying to one who is the son of a slave and was reared in the abolitionist tradition," and went on to point out that "freedom is indivisible, and to attack the Jewish people is to attack the colored." Ignoring Robeson's main thrust against the fascist foes with whom the Allies were at war, the FBI was concerned about only that one aspect of his remarks. Reporting to J. Edgar Hoover, the chief agent in Connecticut (where the Robesons had their home), wrote: "On November 15, 1943, ROBESON made a speech in

Boston, Massachusetts, demanding a full investigation of the recent alleged anti-Semitic incidents in Boston," and the agent "respectfully requested that the Bureau indices be checked for any Communist activity
on the part of PAUL ROBESON." (In FBI reports the subject's name was always capitalized, and any suggestion to the imperious director had to be
made "respectfully.")

It may be noted that in this incident, Robeson was conscious of the guiding spirit of his father—a consciousness that would remain strong
throughout his life. To fulfill his own potential, to serve his own people
while advocating the oneness of mankind, he had to remain true to his
principles regardless of the consequences. As he said, "I had no alternative."

Afterword

ONE DAY PAUL ROBESON SWUNG AROUND from the desk at which he had been working and challenged me to tell him the meaning of the word "truth." I was ahead of time for my appointment with him at his brother's house on 136th Street in Harlem, where he was living in 1953, and for half an hour there had been no sound in the room where he sat, his broad shoulders hunched forward over his writing pad. He had nodded when I entered to let me know that he was aware that I had come, but he continued to write without pause.

His desk faced the windows of his study, the front room of the second floor of the parsonage of Mother A.M.E. Zion Church, which his brother Ben—the Reverend B. C. Robeson—had long served as pastor. Paul was dressed in his usual at-home costume—a shapeless bathrobe of grayish brown, an old pair of trousers, and bare-heeled slippers—that he would not change until his late-evening dinner. From time to time the silence would be broken by the clearing of his throat and then, more of a vibration than a sound, would come the low, tuneless humming that was his habit when lost in the pleasure of his studies.

While waiting I had been browsing among the books that were piled on every surface in the room, and his sudden question startled me. What is truth? As I hesitated, trying to think up something deep as an answer, he prodded me, saying: "Well, what about it? You're a writer, and they say that writers are supposed to be concerned with truth—tell me, what is your definition of that word?"

His manner was that of a rather stern and barely patient high school teacher. It was a manner he sometimes assumed when my daily period of work with him happened to follow his frequent five or six hours of uninterrupted study of one or another foreign language. From previous experience with his Socratic method of teaching by questions I knew that Paul wanted more than some synonyms for "truth," so I stalled for time until I could come up with something close to the answer he had in mind.

In my hand was one of his books of gospel songs, and that gave me an idea. I told Paul that somewhere in the Bible it said that before sentencing Christ to die, Pontius Pilate had demanded that the accused answer that very same question—What is truth—but I didn't remember if the Roman governor had gotten any reply.* So, if Paul had a New Testament handy, I went on, I'd be glad to look it up for him, and I gestured toward the stack of books.

My transparent attempt to evade his question brought a broad smile to his face in place of the frowning intentness, and a quick sidelong glance of comic reproof let me know that he had not missed my "signifying" reference to an innocent man being questioned by an imperious authority. In the flash of his grin he instantly changed roles: The stern instructor now became a chummy upperclassman, eager to share an interesting discovery with a younger student. He beckoned to the desk that was strewn with legal-sized sheets of ruled yellow paper, each of which was covered with vertical rows of ink-drawn Chinese writing.

"Here is the word 'truth,'" he said, pointing to the last of the characters he had written. Then he reminded me that at another time he had shown me how each written Chinese word was an ideograph, a drawing of a particular idea. One example he had demonstrated was the Chinese word for "beggar," which is formed by combining the picture-symbol for "open mouth" with the picture-symbol for "door." Thus, "open mouth at the door" depicts the idea "beggar."

"The word for truth," Paul now told me, was also a combination of several picture-symbols, and then as his ballpoint pen copied the character, he identified each of the various symbols that made up the word. "Here are some wise men," he said, "and here is a height on which they are standing . . . and here they are looking in all directions." (The only part of the complicated word-picture that I remember is the symbol for "all directions," which is made up of two crossed strokes, like a plus sign. Its shape and meaning made me think of the north-south, east-west rods of a barntop weathervane.)

"That, you can see, is 'truth'—isn't it beautiful!" Paul exclaimed, eager for me to share his delight. I agreed that the ideograph was indeed a very

---

* Pilate's question went unanswered (King James Version, John 18:38).

good answer to the question he had asked me. Truth, the word-picture showed us, is that which is found by an intelligent and all-sided view of things; and I marveled that the meaning of the fable about the four blind men and the elephant could be compressed into a single word. However, reminding myself that this was not what we were supposed to be working on, I was careful to do my marveling in silence so as not to repeat the mistake I had made the previous day. Then, my manifest interest in Paul's discussion of the extensive compounding of words in the Hungarian language and certain others had resulted in my spending the entire afternoon trying to follow him on a wide-ranging tour of comparative linguistics during which any glint of enlightenment on my part spurred Paul to plunge with renewed zest deeper and wider into the subject, and every puzzled look had caused him to scoop up another handful of books to find examples that would make me understand. His central idea was to demonstrate that various similarities of language structure and expression indicated the essential kinship of all peoples. Somehow we got to Japan, and one of the things that stuck in my swimming head was that in Japanese there is a doubled word that literally translates as "done done," meaning "have done" as in our Negro spiritual "O Lord, I done done/I done done what you told me to."

It had been fascinating and fun, and even if I had not had a longtime interest in words I could not have helped being spellbound by that virtuoso performance of a consummate actor playing the real-life role of teacher of a subject he passionately loved. But today must be different, I told myself, and I closed the Chinese textbook he had handed me and said: "OK, Paul, I'm convinced. Truth is beautiful in Chinese." The loud unlatching of my briefcase was meant as a sound-symbol for "Please, could we get on to our work now?"

Evidently content on this occasion for me to share his appreciation of only that one gem from the treasure chest of languages, Paul answered my briefcase signal with one of his own. He turned again to his writing pad and began making more copies of that ingenious Chinese character for "truth," thus showing me that business—our business or any other kind—must take second place to his love of learning and his joy in following the trails, in language and in song, that led to the great wonder he had long ago found and yet was ever seeking—the oneness of mankind.

Having made his point, he gathered up the scattered papers on his desk and placed the Chinese language book on the pile of textbooks of the other languages he was currently studying. His large hand was gentle as it rested for a moment upon the books, like a father's hand on the head of a child, and he turned to me and said: "Truth is beautiful in every language."

In the beginning, it all seemed very simple. In 1952, when Paul Robeson asked me to assist him in writing an autobiography, I readily agreed and took a leave of absence from my job as a magazine editor. For the previous three years I had done volunteer publicity work for the Committee to Restore Paul Robeson's Passport, including a widely circulated pamphlet,[1] and was part of a Harlem-based group of Robeson's coworkers led by Alphaeus Hunton, a leader of the Council on African Affairs, of which Robeson was chairman. Prominent in that group was Louis Burnham, an eloquent young man who had been active in the radical Frederick Douglass Club at City College, later was an organizer in Atlanta for the Southern Negro Youth Congress, and was now editor of *Freedom*, a publication that termed itself "Paul Robeson's Paper."

It was Hunton and Burnham who persuaded a reluctant Robeson to write an autobiography, and they told me that Paul had given three reasons for wanting me to be his collaborator. First, I was an African American writer. Second, I shared his political viewpoint. Third, and just as important, I shared his concern to preserve and develop our people's culture. Robeson had warmly endorsed a novel I had published the previous year as being a true picture of the black community,[2] and he liked my outlook on black literature as expressed in various essays and book reviews in *Masses & Mainstream*, of which he was a contributing editor.

As we started, Paul suggested that we leave the assembly of documentary material to a later time: My first task, he said, was to learn what he was like, to try to see him as he saw himself. But that was the rub. It soon became clear that our talk sessions usually digressed to other subjects not only because of Robeson's varied interests but because there was a contradiction between my probing questions and his deeply private nature. And then in the months that followed, during which we worked on a number of other projects (some of them having nothing to do with writing), he became firmly convinced that our eventual work on his life story required of us a many-sided association—in work, in meeting people, in travel. That preparatory phase went on for years, while the writing of his book was, to Paul's gratified relief, postponed indefinitely.

On the team of Robeson's coworkers, my role became much like a utility player on a baseball club—to play at any and all vacant positions. Along with my task of assisting Paul with his newspaper column I was drafted to become director of the newly established Othello Recording Corporation that would share space in the building on Harlem's 125th

Street that housed *Freedom* and the Council on African Affairs. Because the commercial recording companies would no longer reissue Robeson records or make new ones, the demand for his songs could be met only by setting up an independent company. Seed money was raised by people who wanted to overcome the blacklist that was meant to completely silence Robeson.

After we produced our first album, I turned over the operation to Paul Robeson Jr., and sought to get back to our writing project. But there was always something else to be done. Speeches to write. Messages to the many groups in the world who requested them from Paul for various celebrations. Articles for newspapers and magazines here and abroad. Communications with Robeson passport committees in other countries, like that in Britain, which was widely supported by members of Parliament, labor leaders, and many prominent figures in the arts and sciences. And answers to a flood of letters, some drafted for Paul's signature and many others signed by me as his secretary.

For the few months that I was busy making and selling phonograph records, I got a subsistence salary. But for most of my five years' full-time work with Paul I was supported by occasional loans from friends of each of us and mainly by my nighttime employment as a typographical worker at Wall Street financial printers, book houses, and daily newspapers. My hours were just right for work with Paul, who, from his years in the theater, preferred to sleep late and start his day in early afternoon. Then too, I could readily take time off from those jobs to travel with Paul.

And what traveling we did! Blacklisted by all concert agencies, Paul sang throughout the country in black churches and trade union halls. Strenuous efforts were made by the FBI to block these appearances by inducing banks to threaten mortgage foreclosures against sponsoring churches and by pressuring insurance companies to warn of policy cancellations. Audiences were intimidated by the sight of agents copying license-plate numbers of those who came by car.

The subject of these harassments came up when Robeson in 1952 was a guest of Albert Einstein at his home on Mercer Street in Princeton and spent the afternoon talking of many things that Paul would recall in his next newspaper column.[3] When told that we were doing biographical research in the city that was Paul's birthplace, the eminent physicist shook his head in mock wonderment and said to Paul, "You were born here, really. Imagine that!" Then he looked up from the cot on which he was reclining and a mischievous smile lifted his droopy white mustache as he added, "I didn't know anyone was ever *born* here. I thought that Princeton was only a place where people *died!**

When Einstein asked Paul to let him know if he would appear in another Princeton concert, Paul as usual said nothing about the repression he was undergoing. But I couldn't let it go, and I told our host and his assistant, Helen Dukas, about the FBI campaign to silence Robeson and mentioned the copying of license-plate numbers of concertgoers. Whereupon Einstein turned to Ms. Dukas, who was serving us tea and cookies, and said, "Well, Helen, I think it might be safe for us to attend. We don't have a car." He kept a straight face as the rest of us chuckled at the incongruous notion that the world-renowned Dr. Einstein could walk incognito into a Robeson concert in Princeton.

When I remarked to Paul later that I wondered what the FBI, who always had him under surveillance, thought of his visiting a man popularly considered to be the father of the atom bomb, I had no idea that the FBI had kept tabs on Einstein for the previous thirty years.[4] Among the numerous so-called subversive activities of Albert Einstein noted by J. Edgar Hoover's agency was his sponsorship of the American Crusade to End Lynching, which saw Robeson in 1946 lead a delegation to President Harry Truman in the White House for that cause.[5]

Very heartwarming for Paul in those beleaguered years were the annual concerts at Peace Arch Park on the U.S.-Canadian border between the state of Washington and British Columbia. Sponsored by the Mine, Mill, and Smelter Workers, these concerts made it possible for tens of thousands of Canadians to hear Paul sing despite our government's ban on his travel to their country. As I glanced across the border at the vast Canadian audience from my new job as page-turner for accompanist Alan Booth on the breezy outdoor platform, I mentally cheered our "un-American" neighbor country and gratefully remembered that Canada had been a sanctuary for runaway slaves and a safe meeting place for one of America's greatest subversives, Captain John Brown.

Whenever possible I used to stand in the wings where Robeson sang and watch the glistening expressions on his listeners' faces. Whether they were white people like those Canadians or blacks in South Side Chicago or of mixed colors at union-sponsored events, the transforming power of the man's artistry—the velvety lushness of his voice, the magnetism of his

---

* Albert Einstein, who was seventy-three at the time, died three years later in Princeton, where he had lived and worked during the last twenty-two years of his life as an exile from Nazi Germany.

personality—worked a magic spell. The people seemed to like themselves more and to like each other more, and to revel in the experience. Alexander Pope could have been thinking of Paul when he wrote:

> *To wake the soul by tender strokes of art,*
> *To raise the genius, and to mend the heart;*
> *To make mankind in conscious virtue bold,*
> *Live o'er each scene and be what they behold.*

There was a church concert in Boston where I stood in the wings uncomfortably close to a police sergeant on riot duty. Gray-haired, purpled-nose, he held his nightstick in both hands beneath his ample belly. "What a mean bastard," I thought as I warily watched his face. Then I saw him blinking his eyes, his club-holding hands not free to wipe away the tears that flowed down his cheeks as Paul sang "Danny Boy," the Irish folk song about a love that would endure "in sunshine and in shadow" beyond the grave.

Less happy moments were trips to a federal court in Washington, D.C. (passport denial upheld), and to a conference at the State Department in August 1955, where a demand was made for Paul's right to travel to places not requiring a passport. Not long after that conference, limited freedom was granted, and I became manager for concerts in Toronto and Sudbury, Ontario. When Robeson, Alan Booth, his accompanist, and I returned after two weeks of liberation, the U.S. customs officer said, with a leering wink, "Well, I guess you colored boys had a good time up there." We were home again.

Throughout all these activities, I was troubled that during the five years that had elapsed since I left my job as a magazine editor not a line of the projected Robeson autobiography had been written. Whenever the subject came up Paul would refer to the eventual publication as "your book." I would invariably protest that I was not supposed to be his biographer: "Oh no, Paul. I agreed to help you with *your* book, remember?" Then we compromised: It became simply "the book."

Finally, in 1957 we got around to writing "the book" and in November Paul signed the author's foreword of *Here I Stand,* a small volume that was partly autobiographical and a forthright statement of his controversial views. Now I switched from literary collaborator to publisher and promoter, as the Othello Recording Corporation became Othello Associates, which issued the book during Negro History Week the following February.

Not long after that event came Monday, June 16, 1958, when the U.S. Supreme Court ruled in a related case that Robeson could not be compelled to swear he was not a Communist in order to leave the country. After eight years of being silenced as an artist at home and not permitted to accept the many professional offers that came to him from abroad, Paul lost no time in getting his passport and soon departed for London.

O happy day! I rushed back from the airport to tell the story of his getaway to one of Paul's best friends. That was Benjamin J. Davis Jr., a Georgia-born graduate of Amherst and Harvard Law School, talented amateur violinist, former city councilman, and one of the leaders of the Communist Party convicted of violating the unconstitutional Smith Act. Three years had passed since Davis finished a five-year prison term to which he had been sentenced by Judge Harold Medina, who had been one of Robeson's teachers at Columbia.

The joy that Ben and I shared that day at his Riverside Drive apartment was duly noted, if somewhat inaccurately, by the FBI, which, as we always assumed, had bugged the place. In a report to J. Edgar Hoover, later obtained under the Freedom of Information Act, his New York office said it had been "advised on 7/10/58, that BEN DAVIS was visited on that date at his residence by LLOYD BROWN. BROWN, apparently intoxicated, kept shouting, 'That Negro got away, he got away.' (BROWN evidently referring to trip by PAUL ROBESON to Europe.) DAVIS made the statement, apparently referring to ROBESON, 'The Negro from the chain gang made it.'"

It is true that I arrived intoxicated, but I was drunk not from liquor but with joy; and there was nothing there to drink since Ben, alas, didn't use the stuff. (At our house, we always had bourbon for Paul and ginger ale for Ben.)

Noting Robeson's departure the previous day, the *New York Times* of July 11 reported that he said he would give concerts in Europe, including Czechoslovakia and the Soviet Union. When asked if he planned to stay abroad, "Mr. Robeson replied: 'This is my land, My grandfather and father were born here, too, and I don't plan to leave it.'"

During his stay abroad, Robeson's health broke down, and he was treated in hospitals in London, Moscow, and Berlin. Paul was notorious for not writing to friends, and so I was not disappointed that I heard from him only once, in 1962, when he sent me a Christmas card from London. It depicted a man writing a letter, and there was a printed caption that was unintentionally ironic on a card coming from Paul: "A man, Sir," said Doctor Johnson, "should keep his friendship in constant repair." Paul's brief handwritten message was that he was feeling much better after a long illness and that he missed us and hoped to see us soon. (Later, it amused me to put that communication as the only document in a file marked "The Lloyd Brown Collection of Letters from Paul Robeson, 1945–1976.")

After his return in December 1963, we exchanged visits from our nearby homes in Washington Heights, but only once could I induce him to follow his doctor's orders and go for a walk. Under pressure from many sources for a Robeson comment on public affairs, we prepared a statement for release on August 28, 1964, the first anniversary of the March on Washington. In that statement, which as Paul specified was "to the Negro Press Only," he said, "While I must continue my temporary retirement [for reasons of health] . . . my heart has been filled with admiration for the many thousands of Negro freedom fighters and their white associates who are waging the battle for civil rights throughout the country and especially in the South."[6]

Eight months later, on April 22, 1965, Robeson made his first public appearance, which would prove to be his last in New York, at a Welcome Home fund-raiser sponsored by *Freedomways*, a black quarterly dedicated to the civil rights movement. More than 2,000 persons attended the four-hour-long affair presided over by the actor Ossie Davis, who along with fellow actor John Randolph had campaigned in Actors Equity for Paul's right to travel. The program also featured such staunch supporters as Pete Seeger and Hope R. Stevens, Harlem lawyer and activist.

As one who had been satisfied always to remain backstage in Robeson's public life, and by my own wish never sharing any byline credits for our joint work on his many writings, I was pleased on this occasion to have a moment in the spotlight. In his remarks Robeson said, "I would like for a moment to call your attention to two artists who have been closely associated with me in my career." Expressing the hope that Lawrence Brown was still present (he wasn't, having been unable to last through the four-hour program that preceded the introduction of the guest of honor), Paul paid tribute to "my friend and colleague, Mr. Lawrence Brown, an authority on Negro and classical music who has been my partner in concerts for forty years." He continued: "Also here is a friend and colleague, Mr. Lloyd Brown, distinguished writer who gave me such expert assistance with my work on our fighting Negro paper of the fifties, happily called *Freedom*. . . . [and] invaluable assistance in the organization and writing of the book *Here I Stand*. Lloyd, will you just say hello?"[7] I stood up, waved, and sat down, feeling like some movie extra who had been awarded an Oscar.

Later that year, Paul's wife, Essie, died of breast cancer, and after other arrangements for him failed, he found sanctuary at his sister's home in Philadelphia.* When I saw what perfect shelter that was for him, I came to believe that Paul was right in his long-held belief that for him the right thing would always come to pass. Of all the many who truly loved the man, it was only Marian, a widowed and retired schoolteacher, who was the balm in Gilead his soul required. Along with her care for the brother she adored, Marian was a vigilant protector of the privacy that Paul desired. "You've got to watch out all the time," she said as she told me about how one local friend, a businessman, brought along a photographer to a birthday party to take a picture of himself presenting a check to Paul. She stopped that in a flash.

Another close call came when a member of her church sought to do her brother a favor by bringing him a copy of a local tabloid that featured a full-page photo of Paul's face, with a smaller photo of his son set within the forehead.[8] The accompanying article, titled "The Twilight of an Angry Man," consisted of an interview with Paul Robeson Jr., who was quoted as saying his father had offended the Establishment by "sounding like Eldridge Cleaver," then a leader of the Black Panther Party. "Dad was saying," Paul Jr. told the reporter, "'This system has got to shape up or go down. If it's got to go down, we should get ready for the kill.' He didn't suggest that people pick up guns, but the implication was clear." Marian was glad she had intercepted the paper, knowing that her brother would have been greatly upset had he seen that misrepresentation, and she urged me to tell her nephew not to go around talking as if he were Paul Robeson.

During the last nine years of his life, my wife, Lily, and I visited Paul and Marian several times each month. For the most part, Paul did not want any visitors, and he would show his displeasure at unwanted intrusions by remaining silent, a practice that led some people to think he had become a virtual zombie. But that was not the case with visitors with whom he felt at ease, like Dr. Samuel Rosen and his wife, Helen, and Freda Diamond. Over our years together, Paul had developed a warm relationship with our family, including our two daughters, whom I sometimes brought along.

---

* Located at 4951 Walnut Street, the twelve-room house, which was designated a Pennsylvania historic site in 1992, was later established as the Paul Robeson Historical and Cultural Center by the West Philadelphia Cultural Alliance.

In 1971, in his fourth year in Philadelphia, I suggested to Paul that we arrange to have his *Here I Stand* reprinted for the benefit of the new, militant generation of black Americans who had no knowledge of his liberationist ideas. Paul was pleased when the Beacon Press edition came out, and his autographed inscription became a treasured memento. It read: "To dear Lloyd, with deepest thanks for your understanding and kindness. Hope we can work together again in the effort to help our fellow men. A better future for us all—Paul."

One day he asked me, "What about your book, Lloyd?" I laughed at the reminder of the project we had begun almost twenty years ago, but he was serious. Obviously, with his poor health an autobiography was impossible to think of, and I had never liked the idea of an "as told to" book. So that year I arranged with Lee Lurie, his lawyer, to have exclusive rights to use the Robeson family papers for a biography, entered into a contract with a major publisher, and set to work.

Lily accompanied me to Europe for research at Berlin's Paul Robeson Archive, and in Moscow and London. The interviews used for the present book were the result of our work in New Jersey, Illinois, North Carolina, Pennsylvania, and Washington, D.C. Because Paul always insisted that his father was the most important force in his development, we had to find much more than the few facts known about William Robeson, whose family papers had been destroyed.

We also wanted to verify as much as possible the history and legends of Paul's mother's family, about whom he couldn't care less. At my insistence, there was a mention of the Bustills in *Here I Stand,* and from Marian, who was keenly concerned about that background, we got much useful material. Once, when Marian gave me a studio photograph of their mother, Maria Louisa, together with her sister Gertrude and their father, Charles Bustill—all fair of skin—Paul pointed to the skin of his own wrist and said, "That's the trick. If I had looked like them, I would have been bigger than Clark Gable."

Both Paul and his sister were fascinated by my reports on their father's background in North Carolina and by my tracking down of the unknown story of how William Robeson escaped from slavery. Of special interest were my interviews of two Robersons, one white and one black. The white man was attorney Paul D. Roberson, a short, thin, sharp-faced man of sixty whose grandfather, George O. Robason, was one of the three founders of Robersonville. He declined to shake my hand when I visited him at his Railroad Street office (too much social equality, perhaps), but he was helpful nevertheless in providing the names and addresses of two of Paul's relatives. He was very guarded in talking about his connection with the Robeson I was concerned with, observing that he had admired the famous athlete, actor, and singer "before he turned pink." From other sources, I had reason to believe that Paul Roberson's grandfather had been the slaveowner from whom William Robeson escaped. However, when attorney Roberson told me that he had been in New York when Paul Robeson was playing in *Othello,* I was certain that he was the man of whom Paul had written in *Here I Stand.*

In his book Paul recalled that at that time a stranger approached him in a nightclub (it was Cafe Society), saying he was one of the Robesons of North Carolina and he would like to get together for a friendly chat. The man added, "You see, your father used to work for my grandfather." Paul responded, as politely as he could, "You say my father 'used to work for your grandfather.' Let's put it the way it was. *Your grandfather exploited my father as a slave!*" Then, Paul wrote, "That ended it: and *this* Robeson never did have a chummy chat with *that* one."[9]

The black Roberson I met gave me a handshake that was almost too hearty. A big man like Paul and showing a strong family resemblance, Vernon Roberson was a seventy-two-year-old tobacco warehouseman. Vernon and his sister, Mrs. Carrie Lloyd, who also met with me, were grandchildren of Ezekiel Roberson, an older brother of William, Paul's father. They told me that Ezekiel, who lived until the 1920s, had talked with them about the escape the younger enslaved Robersons had made to the Yankees at New Bern. After Emancipation, Ezekiel and his sister, Margaret, returned to be part of the extended family of Benjamin and Sabra.

I never did learn what happened with William between his work for the Union Army in 1863 and his enrollment four years later in the preparatory class of Lincoln University in Pennsylvania. Marian was thrilled when I showed her and Paul the document I found listing William Robeson as an honor graduate in 1873, but Paul was not excited about that. What else could his adored father have been? For me the documents from Lincoln answered one thing that had puzzled me. When Paul used to tell about his father's tutoring him in Latin and Greek, I wondered how an escaped slave had acquired that knowledge to impart. As the record showed, all Lincoln students had to study the classic languages for each of their four years.

Along with my reports on my book research, I would bring enheartening word about the gradual lifting in the 1970s of the blackout that had been imposed on Robeson during the previous two decades. "More good news!" I would say when I told about various honors that were being given him—some schools named after him, various honorary doctorates awarded, and other displays of public esteem. "Praise the Lord," Marian would say, "after all those mean things people been saying about him." But Paul would be noncommittal, except for one time when I brought a copy of *Ebony,* the most widely circulated African American magazine. The publication reported that a panel of historians had found Paul Robeson to be one of the ten greatest black men in American history.[10] His sister said that the people who treated her brother so mean should now feel ashamed of themselves, but Paul simply said, "Pop would have been pleased."

Although Paul was always graciously pleasant to visitors he wished to see, he seldom wore the smile that was once a feature of his friendly personality, and so Lily and I would try to think up things that might break through his somber reserve. One success was a trick we played on him the day after his seventy-sixth birthday on April 9, 1974. "Guess what, Paul," I said before we settled down to the lavish dinner Marian would insist on serving. "Believe it or not, you made the front-page of yesterday's *New York Times!*" Telling Marian that Paul would need his reading glasses, I unfolded the newspaper and pointed to the bottom of a page-one column. There in tiny type was this message:

HAPPY BIRTHDAY PAUL ROBESON
Love from the Brown family.—ADVT.

The gratified smiles of our hosts were even more fulfilling than the dinner of roast chicken and glazed baked ham and baked yams and collard greens and mashed potatoes with giblet gravy and creamed carrots-and-peas and creamed onions and homemade Parker House rolls and sweet potato pie with whipped cream—all served country-style in platters and bowls along with cut-glass pitchers of iced tea on the stiffly starched lace tablecloth by Marian and a helping club-woman friend from the Reeve Memorial United Presbyterian Church. At a nod from his sister, Paul would say grace, and I would silently pray for strength to do justice to that feast and to resist Marian's hospitable pressure to have second helpings.

One source of keen distress to me in those days when Lily and I were shuttling between New York and Philadelphia was that I could not take Lawrence Brown with us sometimes. Marian, of course, could have her local friends visit as she wished, but Paul Jr., who was managing his father's affairs, insisted that otherwise only persons approved by him could visit, an arrangement he would later say his father had instituted to spare him the embarrassment of turning away would-be visitors. He would not approve of any visits by the man whom he had known in childhood as Uncle Larry, saying that he thought it would disturb his father to have Larry come.

In 1972, five years after Paul had moved to Philadelphia, I found Lawrence Brown very low in spirits at his Harlem apartment. On his recent seventy-ninth birthday, Paul and Marian had each sent him a greeting card and a gift check. I suggested he could send a message of thanks on my tape recorder. This he did, and he concluded by saying: "I would love to come and visit you some time before it is too late. I'm getting too old now to visit people, but I hope I'm going to visit you before my time comes." Two days later, on August 23, I played the message for Paul and his sister, and though I had brought Paul many recorded messages on my visits, this was the first and only time he wanted to record a message in return.

In an obvious effort to counter Larry's despondent mood, Paul's statement was the most optimistic expression I had heard from him since his retirement in 1965.

> What you say, Larry [he began]. Certainly thank you for that message, but it would be much better if you'd just come on down to say hello and have some of that—uh—soda and plus [a reference to Larry's penchant for strong drink]. And I'm going pretty well, and I think we'll make it quite a bit from now on. Don't get discouraged, you know, we've got plenty of time. And I'd like to hear your bass to my tenor. They say you really kick it around, man! And I think we should do a *few* concerts for the folks—let 'em know how it was and how it *can* be. OK, as I'm talking to Lloyd and he's going to bring the message to you. Sis is a little bashful, but she's waiting for you. [Marian had shied away from using the microphone.] We'll get together, that's right, all Browns—Brown-Robeson, and Brown, too [nodding toward Lloyd Brown]. And we'll sing a song for dear old Africa—we'll get to them, too. Take it easy. Take it easy. Don't try too hard, but come on over and see us. Be good.[11]

My daughter Linda, who was with me on that visit, remarked that Larry, a frequent visitor to our house, would be thrilled to hear Paul's words, and I added that readers of my biography would also be pleased to see that despite age, infirmity, and years of separation, Paul and Larry had remained steadfast partners in spirit. Sadly, however, there would be no reunion in Philadelphia. Four months later, on Christmas Day, Lawrence Brown was dead.

Though Paul himself had not appeared in public life for the past eight years, there was a growing interest in the man who had long been black-listed and then immobilized by ill health. The most impressive demonstration of that renewed concern was a gala celebration of Paul's seventy-fifth birthday, held in Carnegie Hall in New York on April 15, 1973. A multimedia program of film clips, slides, and live music was produced by Ralph Alswang and Harry Belafonte, with many stars of the performing arts taking part. Among the speakers were Coretta Scott King, widow of Martin Luther King Jr.; Ramsey Clark, former U.S. attorney general; and Mayor Richard Hatcher of Gary, Indiana. The highlight of the evening was a recorded message from Paul. To his many friends who had not heard his voice for years, it was a thrilling moment, all the more so in view of the rumors that he existed only in body but not in mind, or that he was broken, embittered, and disillusioned. His message told a different story, as the *New York Times* reported:[12]

> "I want you to know I am the same Paul," Mr. Robeson said in his recorded message, "dedicated as ever to the worldwide cause of humanity for freedom, peace, and brotherhood. My heart is with the continuing struggle of my own people ... [for] not only equal rights but an equal share." ... Then, booming out strongly, but in spoken words rather than in song, Mr. Robeson said: "But I keeps laughing instead of crying/I must keep fighting until I'm dying/And Ol' Man River, he just keeps rolling along."*

However, despite that public message, the rumors persisted. His enemies—racists and Red-baiters—promoted the idea that he was hiding out in disgrace because of his sins against the American way of life. Others, who professed to be friends while ever seeking to exploit him, were angry that they were not allowed to see him and would not believe that he wanted to be left alone. Since he would not see any reporters, I suggested in 1975, two years after his last public statement, that I should interview

---

* The composer, Jerome Kern, and the lyricist, Oscar Hammerstein II, dedicated "Ol' Man River" to Paul Robeson. This writer once asked Robeson if he knew whether Hammerstein was disturbed by the changes the singer had made in his lyrics. Paul grinned as he told of meeting Hammerstein during the McCarthy years, when many other former acquaintances were afraid to be seen with him. "Oscar just laughed," he recalled, "put his arm around my shoulder and said my changes were OK with him. He said he would keep his own version, of course, and I could keep mine."

him and let him tell everybody, friend and foe alike, why he wished to re-main in seclusion and whether or not his viewpoint had changed. He agreed, and I wrote the story, "Paul Robeson Today,"* for a national press agency, but before it could be published, Paul suffered a stroke and was hospitalized. Day after day, Marian kept a vigil at his bedside, determined that God should not take him from her.

We last visited our friend on January 21, 1976. He was not conscious, but because Paul had always been pleased when Lily gently held his hand as she sat beside him at Marian's home, she did so now and murmured, "Paul, you know we all love you." I could say nothing. Two days later he was gone.

Various circumstances after his death prevented my completion of a full-length biography. However, now, more than twenty years after I first started as Robeson's literary collaborator, I hope that this small work will provide an understanding of what went into the making of that great American, Paul Robeson—artist and warrior, genius son of the Reverend William Drew Robeson, A.B., M.A., S.T.B., and runaway slave.

---

* See Appendix B, "Last Interview."

Appendix A:
The Proud Bustills

Nothing is known about Paul Robeson's ancestry on his father's side before the birth of his grandfather, Benjamin, around 1820; more information exists on his mother's side, the records of which go back to 1732, when Maria Louisa Bustill's great-grandfather was born a slave in Burlington, New Jersey.

Not far from Burlington, which is located twenty miles north of Philadelphia, is the tiny hamlet of Bustleton, which got its name from a wealthy family named Bustill that formerly owned land in the area.[1] The founder of that family, for whom the Bustleton district of Philadelphia also is named, was Samuel Bustill, an English-born Quaker. Until his death in 1742, Bustill, a lawyer, had been a prominent figure in the Province of West New Jersey, a British colony founded at Burlington in 1677 by Quakers from London and Yorkshire. As Benjamin Franklin noted in his *Autobiography*, "Samuel Bustill, the Secretary of the Province," was one of the "principal People" whose friendship the twenty-two-year-old Philadelphia printer cultivated when he came with his employer to Burlington in 1728 to print paper money for that colony.[2] Bustill was a member of an official committee that was set up, Franklin tells us, "to attend the Press, and take Care that no more Bills were printed than the Law directed. They were, therefore, by Turns, constantly with us."

In the likely event that Bustill was one of the several monitors who, Franklin recalled, "had me to their Houses [and] show'd me much Civility" during his three months' work in Burlington, the young printer would have observed that the servants in the Bustill household were black slaves. Although the first collective antislavery statement made in the American colonies had originated nearby among Pennsylvania Quakers some forty years earlier,[3] the movement against the holding of slaves by members of the Society of Friends had not moved Friend Bustill. The first Quaker

145

protesters had asked in 1688: "And those who steal or rob men, and those who buy or purchase them, are they not all alike?" But Attorney Bustill did not see the law that way, and his election as alderman of Burlington in 1734—six years after Franklin's visit—would indicate that his fellow townsmen shared his attitude. And if the buying of stolen property was not considered a sin when the property was a human being stolen from Africa, the community must also have felt that fornication and adultery were not blameworthy when practiced by a man with his own property, for it must have been known in that small town that Alderman Bustill not only owned slaves but was the father of one of them.

That slave was Cyrus Bustill, Paul Robeson's great-great-grandfather, and his date of birth closely coincided with that of George Washington, "Father of His Country." According to the family history maintained by the descendants of Cyrus Bustill, he was born on February 2, 1732 (in some documents March 17 is given), whereas Washington was born in the Virginia colony on February 22 (February 13 Old Style). Though the two newborn boys also shared the circumstance of being the offspring of slaveholders, their differences were so great that it would seem utterly incredible that they should ever meet man to man. Yet such a meeting may have occurred, as claimed by Cyrus's descendants.

It is not known whether any record of Cyrus as the son of Samuel Bustill was privately kept by Bustill's white descendants, though on at least one occasion (as was shown in Chapter 8) a member of that family acknowledged that word of that paternity had come down to later generations. No mention of Cyrus Bustill's parentage was made in a notable account of the black Bustill's family history written by Cyrus's great-granddaughter, Anna Bustill Smith, and published in a scholarly journal in 1925.[4] That writer, who was known as "Cousin Anna" to Paul Robeson (she was his mother's first cousin), alluded to her ancestor's slave-born status when she wrote that Cyrus, "who always championed the cause of freedom and gave of his means to promote it," did not marry young because he "would not perpetuate a race of slaves."

However, Mrs. Smith's daughter, Virginia Bustill Rhetta, was not inhibited on the subject when she wrote a later account of their family. As she put it, "Samuel Bustill . . . an eminent New Jersey lawyer . . . was the father of Cyrus Bustill," and "Cyrus's mother was an African woman stolen from her native land when young, and sold into slavery, and he, according to the laws and customs of slavery, was born a slave."[5]

The earliest documentary record of Cyrus is the mention of him in a will written by Samuel Bustill three years before his death.[6] In addition to his other property, Bustill's last testament, dated May 29, 1739, and probated on October 7, 1742, provided for the disposition of his five household slaves. The will left "my Negroe Girl named Dina" to Bustill's daughter, Sarah Ann; "my Negroe Woman Parthenia" to his wife, Grace; "my Negroe Child named Hester" to his daughter, Mary; "And my mulato Boy named Cyrus, I give and dispose of unto my wife in Trust, Nevertheless that She give and dispose of him to either one of my Said Daughters at her discretion as their circumstances may require, or Obedience to her deserve"; and finally, "I will that my Negroe Cato be sold and the moneys arising from such sale to be applied in and towards the payment of my Debts."

It seems likely that these slaves composed a family unit, with Cato* and Parthenia the parents of Dina and Hester, and Parthenia the mother of her owner's son, Cyrus. That unstated paternal relationship is suggested by the fact that Cyrus was half white and that Bustill wished to hand him down within the family.

Cyrus was ten years old when Samuel Bustill died. No original documents have been found as to his subsequent disposition, but the records kept by his family show that he became apprenticed to a local baker and paid for his freedom by his work at that trade. Virginia Bustill Rhetta, the most recent family chronicler, gives this account of his emancipation:

> At the death of his father and master in 1742, he learned he was to be sold. He abhorred slavery and appealed to a Quaker baker, Thomas Pryor† of Burlington. He bound himself to him and promised to repay the price after learning the business, and he did. Thomas Pryor was a friend of Samuel Bustill and knew the lad was his son, so he bought Cyrus, and took him to his home. Cyrus attended Quaker schools and meetings. A boy was paid to teach him while the bread was baking. He learned the business and opened a bakery for himself. . . . The records show Cyrus Bustill conducted his bread and cake business many years with credit and profit.[7]

---

* The common practice of giving slaves distinguished names like Cato, Caesar, Brutus, and Pompey was evidently gratifying to the early American slaveowner. What other mere mortal could command even a Jupiter to do his bidding?

† According to Anna Bustill Smith's account, Pryor's bakery may have been located on "one of the streets running to the fast flowing Delaware [that] was named for him." Now eliminated by a waterfront redevelopment project, Pryor's Alley is shown on city maps to have extended from Pearl to Delaware Streets in the block between Stacy and York Streets.

In the transfer of Cyrus to Pryor, it is not known whether Bustill's widow, who inherited Cyrus, simply wanted to get rid of her husband's son by an African woman or made the move with the boy's future welfare in mind. A benevolent motive on Grace Bustill's part is suggested by the fact that Cyrus later named one of his daughters Grace.

As a free if not equal man who achieved success as a tradesman, Cyrus Bustill was typical of former slaves who managed to purchase their freedom: The achievement of raising themselves from chattel to man gave them an extra measure of self-esteem over that which is usual with other "self-made" men. The independent spirit of the founder of the proud black Bustill family is illustrated by the following anecdote from a family history published around 1890:

> In [Cyrus's] day it was regarded as a great insult for the humble in life or the lowly in station to drive past the rich and dignified upon the public road. And the insult was considered greatly aggravated if the offender happened to be colored and presumed to own and drive his own horse.
>
> Cyrus Bustill possessed a very fine and spirited horse and was very fond of a fast drive. It so happened that upon one very warm and sultry afternoon, upon a very dusty road while enjoying a ride in the country that he caught up to the judge and his family, likewise enjoying a ride in the family carriage. Soon tiring of the dust and the slow pace of the judge's horses, he turned out and gave his horse the rein. And as he was dashing past the carriage the judge looked out to see who dared to thus insult him and his family upon the public road. And when he recognized the horse and his master, he roared out with great indignation, "Cyrus, fetch me no more bread." "Very well, Judge," replied the baker as he disappeared in the dust.
>
> He discontinued the serving of the bread and supposed that the assertion of his manhood and the exercise of his rights upon the public highway had cost him his best customer. But the judge's family, after waiting until they were satisfied from the well known character and principles of this colored Quaker baker that he neither intended to apologize for what he could not regard as an insult, nor solicit a renewal of their custom after he had been ordered in unmistakable manner and language to stop the usual morning serving of bread, recognized his manhood and his rights by renewing their numerous orders for his good bread, biscuits and cakes. And the judge, who was highly respected for his sound judgment and honest convictions, was ever afterward his firm friend and generous customer.[8]

On April 29, 1773, when he was forty-one, Cyrus married Elizabeth Morrey, who like himself was of a racial mixture. Her father, Richard Morrey, was an Englishman, and her mother, named Satterthwait, was a member of the Leni-Lenape tribe of Indians.* Thus the eight children who were born to Cyrus and Elizabeth were a mixture of African, European, and indigenous American stock, and by the racial mores of the country—in 1773 as in 1993—they were denoted as blacks. Two girls were born to the couple prior to the Declaration of Independence; two more girls were born during the Revolutionary War; a fifth girl and then three boys were born in the new nation that was "conceived in liberty and dedicated to the proposition that all men are created equal."

During the Revolution, Cyrus worked at his trade in Burlington and, as the story has come down in his family, rendered valuable help to the American cause by baking bread for Washington's starving troops in their ordeal at Valley Forge in the winter of 1777–1778. For that patriotic service—the story goes on—Cyrus was given a silver coin by General Washington, and the coin was handed down through successive generations of Bustills.[9] The plethora of legends about George Washington may justify skepticism concerning that account. Nevertheless, the story is plausible: Bread *was* delivered at times to Valley Forge, and Burlington, a port on the Delaware River, was only about sixty miles from that encampment. Furthermore, there is documentary evidence that Cyrus Bustill did in fact bake bread for the Continental Army, for which he received official commendation. Consequently, if the commander-in-chief gave that coin to Cyrus, the award was merited. A certificate, treasured by his descendants, was given to Cyrus six months after the war ended. It reads:

> I hereby certify that Cyrus Bustill has been employed in the baking of all the flour used at the port of Burlington and that he has behaved himself as a faithful, honest man and has given satisfaction such as should recommend him to every good inhabitant.
>
> Given under my hand at Burlington, May 1st. 1782
>
> (Signed)
> Thomas Falconer
> Contractor for supplying troops at the above mentioned port.[10]

Soon after the war Cyrus and his family moved to Philadelphia, where he opened a bakery at 56 Arch Street. Then the largest community in the United States, the City of Brotherly Love also had a large black popula-

---

* The Leni-Lenape (the name means "real man") were a branch of the Algonquin Indians. Better known by the misnomer Delaware, the Leni-Lenape made a peace treaty with William Penn in 1683 concerning Quaker settlement in the area.

tion that numbered, in 1790, more than 10,000, of whom some 3,700 were slaves. The city was then the political and cultural center of the country, and its black community, of which Cyrus became an active member, was the most influential and progressive of any at the time. Cyrus was a founding member of the Free African Society, a mutual-aid organization formed by Philadelphia blacks in 1787, which "by 1790 devoted itself to antislavery agitation, the prevention of Negro kidnaping, and cooperation with other emancipationist groups."[11]

Later when the Free African Society was reorganized as the First African Church, the "colored Quaker baker" could not break with his creed and go along with that development, which established on July 28, 1791, one of the first independent black churches in America.* However, his helpful role in that history-making beginning was cited in that church's records. After describing Cyrus as being "generally respected for his uprightness, and much relied upon by his brethren for his sound judgment," the historian noted that "He was the first to relinquish his [financial] claim in the old [Free African] Society in behalf of the church. This noble act appears to good advantage in view of his religious sentiments, which accorded with those of the Friends."[12]

When he retired from business around 1790, Cyrus opened a school for black children in his home, thereby becoming the first of a line of Bustill schoolteachers that continued down to Maria Louisa, Paul Robeson's mother. The most notable continuer of that vocation was Sarah Mapps Douglass, a truly remarkable woman who for sixty years taught several generations of black children in Philadelphia. Sarah, who was born in 1806—the year Cyrus died—was the daughter of Cyrus's daughter Grace, who had married a "highly respected, scholarly, Christian man" named Robert Douglass.[13] (The light-skinned, educated, middle-class Bustills generally married their counterparts in the black community.) Sarah also continued the family's abolitionist tradition started by Cyrus by becoming a founding member of the Philadelphia Female Anti-Slavery Society and the National Anti-Slavery Convention of American Women.

Sarah Douglass did not, however, continue her family's attachment to the Society of Friends, and she may have been the first of the Bustills to break away. In 1837, four years after she stopped attending the Arch

---

* Richard Allen, who initiated the Free African Society and later founded the African Methodist Episcopal Church, is generally considered to be the father of the black-controlled church, historically the center of African American community life. Like Cyrus Bustill, Bishop Allen had purchased his freedom.

Street meeting* (which Grandfather Cyrus had attended and to which her mother still belonged), Sarah explained her withdrawal in a letter to a Quaker in England, wherein she noted that

> there is a bench set apart at that meeting for our people, whether *officially* appointed or not I cannot say; but . . . my mother and myself were told to sit there, and that a friend sat at each end of the bench to prevent white persons from sitting there. And even when a child my soul was made sad with hearing five or six times during the course of one meeting . . . 'This bench is for the black people.' 'This bench is for the people of color.' And oftentimes I wept, at other times felt indignant and queried in my own mind are these people Christians.[14]

Racism was still strong among the Philadelphia Quakers, she reported, though there were "a 'noble few,' who have cleansed from their garments the foul stain of prejudice."[15]

Two years later, Sarah's brother, Robert Douglass Jr., was all packed for a trip to England for further instruction in his profession of portrait painter. He was taking with him a "letter of introduction from Thomas Sully who crossed the Atlantic to take a portrait of Queen Victoria." But sadly, as a white abolitionist friend of Sarah's noted in a letter, "her brother had been refused a passport to England on account of his color, the Secretary of State alleging that by the new Constitution of Pennsylvania the people of color were not citizens and therefore had no right to passports to foreign countries"; and as for Robert, "He writhes under our wicked prejudice."[16] Nevertheless, that American-born noncitizen, whose grandfather had helped to win the nation's independence, did go to London, for passports were not then a legal requirement for departure or reentry.[†] (More than a century later another secretary of state would refuse a passport to Robert Douglass's grandnephew, Paul Robeson, alleging among other things that Robeson was too actively opposed to that same "wicked

---

* That place of worship, the Friends Meeting House, was erected in 1804 at Fourth and Arch Streets and is still used by the local Quakers.

† In their struggle for equal rights, free blacks included the demand for passports both as a proof of citizenship and a necessity for travel in certain countries. William Wells Brown, a fugitive slave and abolitionist leader who pressed that issue, scornfully observed that though it was the age of discovery, "none but an American slaveholder could have discovered that a man born in a country was not a citizen of it" (*The Liberator*, November 30, 1849).

prejudice." In Robeson's case, however, the denial of his passport made it unlawful for him to depart.)

The direct line to Paul Robeson is traced from Sarah's and Robert's uncle, David Bustill, who was the last-born (in 1788) of Cyrus Bustill's children. David, who became a plasterer and taught that trade to two of his sons, was, like his parents and brothers and sisters, devoutly attached to the Quaker faith. And like other religious abolitionists he stoutly believed that to oppose slavery was to do God's work, a view expressed by this February 1, 1856, entry in his diary: "This day the Lord sent me to the Court House, under the steeple at the center building, to warn the court not to do anything more against us, they having a man claimed to be a fugitive slave."[17] His granddaughter later would write that at David Bustill's "stern denunciation of the injustice . . . the court seemed spellbound and listened till he departed. The judge then released the man."[18]

David Bustill, who died in 1866 at the age of seventy-eight, had lived to see the overthrow of the ungodly slave system. The second of the nine children born of his marriage to his cousin, Mary Hicks, was Charles Hicks Bustill—Paul Robeson's grandfather. Charles, who was born in 1816, and his older brother, James Mapps Bustill, became partners as plastering contractors with their father who had worked at that trade for forty years.

But though they followed their father's line of work, Charles and James—as well as their younger brother, Joseph Casey Bustill, who became a schoolteacher—did not continue as Quakers. Doubtless they shared their cousin Sarah Douglass's indignation at the prejudice that prevailed in the Society of Friends. And, though the Quakers were by far the most liberal white denomination in the country, there now existed independent black churches wherein no child would ever weep for being treated as an inferior. Together with his brother James, Charles Bustill joined the First African Presbyterian Church,* which he served for many years as chairman of its board of trustees.

However, Charles and his brothers did remain faithful to the family's social doctrine, all three becoming ardent abolitionist leaders in the Philadelphia black community, which was in the forefront as a center of

---

* The First African Presbyterian Church developed from the original, nondenominational First African Church (mentioned earlier) as did the first churches of two other black denominations—the African Protestant Episcopal and the African Methodist Episcopal.

antislavery activity. Thus James M. Bustill played a prominent part in one of the most militant of the nationwide mass meetings that protested the proslavery Dred Scott decision. Under the heading "SPIRITED MEETING OF THE COLORED CITIZENS OF PHILADELPHIA," the abolitionist paper, *The Liberator*, reported a "large meeting of colored people [held on April 3, 1857] in Israel Church ... to consider the atrocious decision of the Supreme Court in the Dred Scott case, and the other outrages to which colored people are subjected under the Constitution of the United States. The meeting was organized by the appointment of James M. Buctel [misprint for "Bustill"] as chairman."[19]

(A resolution adopted at that rally asserted that because the government's highest tribunal had declared that Negroes had no rights that had to be respected, Negroes in turn owed no allegiance to that government. That concept, in another form, would make headlines a century later in a national controversy involving James Bustill's grandnephew, Paul Robeson.)

The main antislavery activity in Philadelphia (where slavery no longer existed) was the rescue of fugitive slaves from the bordering slave states of Delaware, Maryland, and Virginia (the part that is now West Virginia) as well as runaways from farther south. Directing that work, which flouted the federal Fugitive Slave Act, was the General Vigilance Committee, set up in 1852 and "composed of persons of known responsibility ... who could be relied upon to act systematically and promptly" in behalf of fugitives.[20] Charles H. Bustill, Paul Robeson's grandfather, was one of the seven African Americans elected to that nineteen-member body. Under the leadership of the black abolitionist William Still, that committee was one of the most effective of such groups in the country, aiding the escape—to cities farther north and to Canada—of 465 slaves in the first four years of its existence.

While Charles Bustill was serving on what might be called the board of directors of one of the busiest terminals of the Underground Railroad, his younger brother, Joseph, was one of that line's most active shipping agents. In Harrisburg, Pennsylvania, where he had gone to teach school, Joseph took charge of that important transfer point for runaways. An excerpt from one of the first "business" letters he sent to William Still in Philadelphia showed that the new agent had much to learn about how to convey information concerning the illegal work he had embarked upon. In that message, dated March 24, 1856, to "Friend Still" in Philadelphia, he wrote:

I suppose ere this you have seen those five large and three small packages I sent by way of Reading, consisting of three men and women and children. They arrived here this morning at 8 $\frac{1}{2}$ o'clock and left twenty minutes past three. . . . Lately we have formed a Society here, called the Fugitive Aid Society. This is our first case, and we hope it will prove entirely successful. When you write please inform me what signs or symbols you make use of in your dispatches, and any other information in relation to operations of the Underground Rail Road.[21]

No doubt Friend Still advised Joseph to be less explicit when violating federal law, and a later message was properly cryptic:

Harrisburg, May 31st, 1856

Wm. Still, N. 5th St.:—I have sent via [sic] at two o'clock four large and two small hams.

Jos. C. Bustill[22]

In William Still's classic account, *The Underground Rail Road,* we learn that the listed items—four adults and two children—were hotly pursued runaways from Maryland; and the author related with obvious relish that when a couple of white men tried to stop the fugitives on the road to Pennsylvania, the two young men in the party "struck away at them with all their might, with their large clubs, not even waiting to hear what those superior individuals wanted. The effect of the clubs brought them prostrate in the road, in an attitude resembling two men dreaming (it was in the night)."[23]

No documentary record exists as to the total number of slaves rescued by the dedicated Harrisburg agent in the seven years he did that voluntary work, but the number was large. Joseph Bustill's daughter recalled that she "often heard him say he helped over a thousand fugitives to safety."[24]

Joseph Bustill's marriage at Gettysburg to Sarah Humphrey brought another infusion of Native American stock into the family, his bride having been born into the Chippewa tribe at their village near Niagara Falls, New York. The granddaughter of the couple wrote that Sarah "could not return to her tribe after marrying a colored teacher, but once a year was sent gifts from her parents."[25]

In 1863—during the Civil War—Joseph returned to Philadelphia, where he taught school for another ten years (he had taught for ten years in Wilmington, Delaware, and ten more in Harrisburg), and then retired to a large house he had built in the town of Lincoln University, Pennsylvania, about forty miles west of Philadelphia. Lincoln University was a school for black men, established in 1854 by the white Presbyterian denomination, and many of its students—including a number from Africa—roomed and boarded at the twenty-two-room Bustill house. (The enterprising owner also operated a store in that house, and on one occasion he was charged with selling whisky without a license as well as "cider so strong that students at the University felt dizzy just after tasting it." At his trial the defendant denied both charges and—happily for the honor of the proud Bustills—he was acquitted.)[26]

Naturally no undignified incident like that would ever be mentioned by Anna Bustill, the future family historian who lived with her parents in that bustling and certified-sober ménage. Anna, who became still another Bustill schoolteacher, was often visited by two of her cousins from Philadelphia, who were also teachers. Those two young women, who were daughters of Charles Bustill and his wife, Emily Robinson, were Maria Louisa, born in 1853, and Gertrude Elizabeth, who was two years younger.

Fortunately for this story, one of the Lincoln graduates of the Class of 1873—which was the year Joseph Bustill moved to that college town—decided to continue his studies at the university's three-year theological department. That student's name was William Drew Robeson, and it must be assumed (there being no documentation for it) that it was at Lincoln that he met Maria Louisa, his future wife and the mother of their seven children, the last of whom was Paul Robeson.

Before ending this summary of the Bustill side, note must be taken of Paul Robeson's Aunt Gertrude, his mother's only sibling. Aunt Gertrude was the only close Bustill relative still living when Paul was growing up. Grandfather Charles had died in 1890, eight years before Paul was born, and Grandmother Emily, many years earlier. Described as a person of great energy and versatility, Gertrude Bustill was an outstanding representative of the socioeconomic group that styled itself "the better class of colored people." If not "better" than others, they were nevertheless very good, as the lives and works of Gertrude and her distinguished husband demonstrated.

Like Paul Robeson's mother, Gertrude married a Lincoln University graduate whom she probably met on that campus about the time her sister met William Robeson. He was Nathan Francis Mossell ("Uncle Frank" to Paul), who was born in Canada of freeborn parents from Baltimore who returned to the United States after slavery was abolished. After getting his A.B. at Lincoln, Mossell became the first black graduate of the University of Pennsylvania Medical School; and later he founded in Philadelphia the Frederick Douglass Memorial Hospital and Training School for Nurses, which he served for nearly forty years as medical director. Because that hospital, which still exists, received no public funds at the time, an important responsibility fell upon Gertrude Mossell and the women's auxiliary she formed to help raise the money to maintain that vital institution for the black community.

One field of work was not enough for the driving ambition of Mrs. Mossell, who was also the mother of two daughters (who would in time produce four more Bustill schoolteachers). The byline "Mrs. N. F. Mossell" began to appear on numerous columns and articles in various black newspapers and magazines—and some white ones, too—as Gertrude sought by her writings to advance the cause of her people. When a book entitled *The Work of the American Woman,* which purported to present the contributions made to the country by women, failed to mention one who was black, the spirited Bustill woman responded with a book of her own—*The Work of the Afro-American Woman.*[27]

In her book, first published in 1894, Mrs. Mossell recounted the achievements of black women from the poet Phyllis Wheatley (1753–1784) to her own time, rating highest the "philanthropic work" of abolitionists like Harriet Tubman and Sojourner Truth. Then she listed the names of contemporary black women who were active in the fields of education, journalism, medicine, law, religion, the arts, and invention. (The last entry among the inventors was this: "Mrs. N. F. Mossell of Philadelphia has invented a camping table and portable kitchen.") Not stopping with the achievements of her own class, the author also paid tribute to the industrious black women in the South, "who hoe, rake, cook, wash, chop, patch and mend from morning until night . . . and there are many cases where the wife is a much better 'cotton chopper' than her husband."

Mrs. Mossell's husband, who was cited by his community as "an uncompromising champion of racial justice," had been a member of the first executive committee of the National Association for the Advancement of Colored People. Dr. Mossell was a warm admirer of Paul Robeson, and on one occasion late in life he told one of his granddaughters (another Bustill teacher): "If you have never been called a 'radical,' 'Red,' 'Communist,' 'Bolshevik,' etc.—depending on the era in which you live—you should begin to examine your conscience. It means that you have never done anything for anyone but yourself."[28]

In 1947, a year after her husband's death at the age of ninety, the tireless work of Gertrude Mossell ended at the age of ninety-two. Her many accomplishments had enriched the legacy of Bustill achievements. She died with the satisfaction of knowing that four of her granddaughters were continuing the family tradition of teaching, and that her sister's daughter, Marian Robeson, had also become a schoolteacher in Philadelphia. Then too she had lived to see her nephew, Paul, become the most notable of all the Bustill line as he won international fame as a concert singer and starring actor on stage and screen. One small regret may have troubled Aunt Gertrude at the end: Despite her persistent entreaties, Paul had for years stubbornly refused on principle to attend the reunions she used to organize, where all of her kin would gather to hear recited the history—beginning with Cyrus in 1732—of the proud Bustills in America.

Appendix B:
Last Interview

While arrangements were being made with a national news service for the publication of the following interview, Paul Robeson's health took a turn for the worse. After suffering a stroke, he was hospitalized on December 28, 1975, and died on January 23, 1976.

PAUL ROBESON TODAY
By Lloyd L. Brown
Philadelphia, October 18, 1975

As he rises with a smile from his easy chair to greet a visitor, it can be seen that Paul Robeson no longer has the massive physique that was so impressive to audiences when he was a famous black actor playing Othello or singing "Ol' Man River" in *Show Boat*. Nor is there any sign of the dynamic power of the legendary "Robeson of Rutgers" who once bowled over opposing linemen on college gridirons and later battled against the likes of Jim Thorpe in the bruising encounters of pro football's early years.

Gaunt and gray in his seventy-eighth year, Robeson is dressed for company in a blue serge suit, starched white shirt, and brocaded tie. As he strides toward the vestibule for the welcoming handshake, he squares his shoulders in the jacket that has become too large for him, and he holds himself erect to his full six-foot-three. For a moment the years are rolled back and one recalls how the man used to stand like this after a concert performance, beaming upon and clasping hands with the scores of people who would line up to greet him. "Thanks a million," he would murmur, or, as he says now to his audience of one, "So glad you could come."

But after that gallant effort to enact his former self, he is obviously relieved to get back to his restful chair. To the opening question as to whether he is feeling any better these days, Robeson gives his usual reply: "Just kickin' along." The reference to his health causes the smile to slip from the dark mahogany brown of his face, and his tone conveys his keen regret that he no longer can lead an active life.

For forty years the man was a headline personality, first gaining fame as a football star and then going on to win international acclaim both as a concert bass-baritone and a starring actor of stage and screen. After World War II he emerged as a controversial black militant whose intransigence made him a target of mob attacks, blacklisting, and governmental repression during the McCarthy era. Asserting that "Paul Robeson's travel abroad would be contrary to the best interests of the United States," the State Department denied him a passport for eight years, until the Supreme Court reversed that action.

Typical of Robeson's nonconformist attitude was his vigorous opposition in 1954 to U.S. aid for the French military effort in Vietnam. Prophetically warning against the danger of direct American involvement in that conflict, he said: "I ask again: Shall Negro sharecroppers from Mississippi be sent to shoot down brownskinned peasants in Vietnam—to serve the interests of those who oppose Negro liberation at home and colonial freedom abroad?"

And two years later, when he was haled before the House Committee on Un-American Activities, Robeson defied his inquisitors. Asked why he did not stay in Russia, which he had praised after several visits to that country, Robeson retorted: "Because my father was a slave, and my people died to build this country, and I am going to stay right here and have a part of it, just like you. And no fascist-minded people will drive me from it. Is that clear?"

Ostracized because of his radical views, Robeson was an unknown figure to the ghetto militants and campus rebels of the Sixties who echoed his earlier preachments. And because of his poor health—he has suffered from arteriosclerosis since 1961—he could not be active in the civil rights movement that gave rise to such spokesmen as Martin Luther King Jr., Malcolm X, and others.

For the last ten years Robeson has lived in seclusion at the Philadelphia home of his widowed sister, Mrs. Marian Forsythe, a retired schoolteacher. During that time he has made no public appearances and has firmly denied all requests for interviews. The only visitors he receives are relatives and a few close friends. "I am sorry," he says, "that I must say no to many old friends who want to come, but I am just not up to it."

As he lives out his last years here in Philadelphia, Robeson feels he has come close to his earliest days. He and his sister are the last of the seven children born to William D. Robeson and Maria L. Bustill, who were married nearly a century ago in this city. William Robeson was a runaway slave from North Carolina who had graduated with honors from Lincoln University, and Maria Bustill a local schoolteacher. Their marriage in 1878 took place at the First African Presbyterian Church, which was an outgrowth of the First African Society that had been founded in 1787 by Maria's great-grandfather, Cyrus Bustill, as the nation's first black self-help organization. Then, too, Maria Bustill's father and two uncles had been leaders of the antislavery movement in what was then the most militant of America's black communities.

"In addition to that family background," Robeson told a visiting friend and biographer, "you should know that as a young fellow still in college I was always in and out of Philadelphia, to parties and such." Lowering his voice to a conspiratorial whisper, as if to keep his sister, a devoted church-worker, from hearing, he added: "Place was just full of pretty girls—mmh *mmh!*"

Then he smiled across the dinner table to Marian, who pretended she had not heard that mantalk, and said, "Anyway, it sure is good to be here with Sis—at home."

That home, a twelve-room brick house in a black neighborhood in West Philadelphia, is Robeson's world today. His chronic illness has sapped his strength, and the former global traveler and master of more than a score of languages seldom leaves the house. "I just don't feel up to going out much any more," he told his visitor. "And as for all these invitations I get nowadays—" he threw up his hands to express how utterly impossible it was for him to attend the numerous functions where plaques or scrolls are awarded him for past achievements.

Recent honors have come from such groups as Actors Equity, New York Urban League, Hollywood NAACP, Jewish Cultural Clubs of New York, Black Psychiatrists of America, and Veterans of the Abraham Lincoln Brigade. Honorary doctorates have been bestowed by Rutgers and Lincoln Universities, and Robeson was among the first group of actors selected for Broadway's theater Hall of Fame.

Though he is unable to attend such gatherings, the sick man is gratified that his pioneering efforts for colonial freedom abroad and black equality at home have increasingly become recognized. A notable instance of that vindication was the recent Award of Merit given him by the seventeen-member Congressional Black Caucus, who earlier had greeted him on his birthday with this message: "Without Paul, there would not be us."

A holdout to that trend is the National Football Foundation's Hall of Fame whose officials contend that though Robeson's playing record qualifies him for their roster of college gridiron greats, his later controversial activities make him unacceptable. A recent visitor asked Robeson what he had to say about that exclusion and the efforts now being made by Edward J. Bloustein, Rutgers's president, to have the ban lifted.

In response, the old man merely smiled and shrugged his shoulders. A half-century after his playing days, the two-time All-American, who was said by Walter Camp to be "the greatest end that ever trod the gridiron," sees no reason to comment on the judgment of the Hall of Fame officials.*

Habitually a late-riser—a hangover from his years in the theater—Robeson spends his afternoons and evenings with books, newspapers, and magazines; and there is always a large batch of fan mail for him to read. The letters and cards come from old admirers and from young people who have just learned of his existence and want to hear from him. To let such letters pile up unanswered is another longtime Robeson habit, though now he has the valid excuse of illness. His business mail is attended to by his son and his attorney.

The theater, which diverted him from the legal career he began after graduating from Columbia Law School in 1923, still holds Robeson's interest. He frequently watches plays presented on TV by the local public broadcasting station. Network news programs and special events are also watched as well as an occasional football or basketball game.

Robeson talked about the radical changes that have taken place in football since his own playing days, when the top-ranked Rutgers eleven of 1917 had only nineteen members on the squad and Robeson played every

---

* On January 18, 1995, the National Football Foundation announced that Paul Robeson would be posthumously inducted that year into the College Football Hall of Fame, seventy-six years after the legendary "Robeson of Rutgers" played his last game for that school. The induction took place on August 25, 1995.

minute of that season's nine games. He had no opinion as to whether the modern-style game was better than the old, saying that the differences were too wide to permit comparison.

"But there's one change," he said, "that always delights me—seeing so many of our folks on all the various teams. In the old days—well, not only was I the only black player on our football team, but I can recall only one other player of my color on all the teams we played against for four years. As for professional baseball, it's wonderful to see so many black players after that long, hard struggle it took to get the first one in." (Robeson's modesty, if not his bulk, is as massive as ever, and he makes no mention of the pioneering role he played in that effort, such as his leadership of a delegation in 1944 that pressed the club owners to erase the color line in organized baseball.)

An all-out activist since his college days, when he earned letters in four sports while simultaneously winning top honors in scholarship, Robeson evidently decided to be an all-out retiree when his health broke down.

"When I tried to make a comeback in 1965," he told his visitor, "I found that public appearances were too much of a strain on me. So I came down here to be with Sis and to live a completely private life."

He was reminded that because of the growing interest in him many people want to know what he has to say for himself nowadays. If he would not reconsider his refusal to be interviewed by the press, would he at least be willing to express in writing his views on current affairs?

"Definitely not," Robeson replied. "No interviews and no public statements—that's it. People should understand that when I was active I went here, there, and everywhere. What I wanted to do, I did. What I wanted to say, I said. And now that ill-health has compelled my retirement, I've decided to let the record speak for itself. As far as my basic outlook is concerned, everybody should know that I am the same Paul Robeson, and the viewpoint I expressed in my book, *Here I Stand,* has never changed." In that book, published in 1958, he presented his views on national and international issues.

The consistency of the man's attitude was seen in the most recent of his rare communications. Writing in 1974 [the previous year] to Actors Equity to thank the organization for establishing an annual Paul Robeson Award and making him its first recipient, he concluded:

"It has been most gratifying to me in retirement to observe that the new generation that has come along is vigorously outspoken for peace and liberation, and that the forces of bigotry have received many setbacks. To all the young people, black and white, who are so passionately concerned about making a better world, I say: Right on!"

This writer, who has known the man well for thirty years, can report that Paul Robeson, alive but regrettably not well in Philadelphia, is indeed the same Paul Robeson whom so many remember.

Notes

PREFACE

1. Robeson's speech was made at a Royal Albert Hall antifascist rally, June 24, 1937.

2. Brown's epitaph is based on an excerpt from Robeson's message: "In our sorrow, now that he is gone, let us remember that the creative works of Lawrence Brown will never die."

3. *Here I Stand* (New York: Othello Associates, 1958; reprinted, Boston: Beacon Press, with Preface by Lloyd L. Brown, Introduction by Sterling Stuckey, 1988), p. 2.

4. *Ibid.,* p. 6.

5. *Daily Home News,* New Brunswick, N.J., June 5, 1919.

6. *Masses & Mainstream,* Vol. I, No. 8, October 1948, p. 23.

CHAPTER ONE

1. "Paul Leroy Robeson," *Targum,* Vol. L, No. 30, June 1919, p. 566.

2. "Double Play: Chaplin to Robeson to Malenkov," *Saturday Evening Post,* Vol. 227, No. 4, 1954, pp. 10–12.

3. "Ode to Paul Robeson," in *Salute to Paul Robeson* (New York: unpaged brochure, 1973).

4. Paul Robeson, "I Want to Be African," in E. G. Cousins, ed., *What I Want from Life* (London: George Allen and Unwin Ltd., 1934), p. 71.

5. *Webster's New World Dictionary, College Edition* (New York: World, 1957), p. 1259.

6. Paul Robeson, *Here I Stand,* p. 33.

7. Paul Robeson, "The Culture of the Negro," *The Spectator* (London), June 15, 1934, pp. 916–917.

8. Marie Seton, *Paul Robeson* (London: Dennis Dobson, 1958), p. 43.

9. Lawrence Perry, "Why Does a Winner Win?" *Associated Men of Y.M.C.A.,* Vol. XLV, No. 6, February 1924, p. 248.

10. Eslanda Goode Robeson, *Paul Robeson, Negro* (London: Gollancz, 1930), p. 21.

11. Shirley Graham, *Paul Robeson, Citizen of the World* (New York: Messner, 1946), p. 20.

12. Martin Bauml Duberman, *Paul Robeson* (New York: Knopf, 1988), p. 5.

CHAPTER TWO

1. Paul Robeson, *Here I Stand*, p. 9.

2. Paul Robeson, "Here's My Story," *Freedom*, Vol. II, No. 4, April 1952, p. 5.

3. Speech at Second National Convention of the National Negro Labor Council, Cleveland, Ohio, November 21, 1952. *Freedomways*, Vol. II, No. 1, 1971, p. 116.

4. Interview with Paul D. Roberson, a grandson of George O. Roberson, October 20, 1971, at Robersonville, N.C.

5. Will Book No. 2, pp. 138–139, Martin County Courthouse, Williamston, N.C.

6. *Ibid.*, p. 230.

7. John Hope Franklin, *From Slavery to Freedom* (3rd ed., New York: Knopf, 1967), p. 218.

8. Williamston *Democratic Banner*, August 7, 1856. On microfilm, Department of Archives and History, Raleigh, N.C.

9. William Still, *The Underground Rail Road*, (Philadelphia: Porter and Coates, 1872), pp. 313–317.

10. James H. McCallum, *Martin County During the Civil War* (Williamston, N.C.: Enterprise Publishing Co., 1971), pp. 7, 10.

11. Benjamin Quarles, *The Negro in the Civil War* (Boston: Little, Brown, 1953), p. 92.

12. James H. McCallum, *Martin County During the Civil War*, pp. 132–141.

13. John Hope Franklin, *From Slavery to Freedom*, p. 285.

14. The *Fayetteville* [N.C.] *Observer* reported the depreciation of slave property on January 14, 1861, and the auction sale on November 25, 1861; both citations quoted in James H. Boykin, *North Carolina in 1861* (New York: Bookman Associates, 1961), pp. 44–45.

15. Interview with Francis M. Manning at Williamston, N.C., October 20, 1971. Manning, a retired newspaper editor and publisher whose mother was a Roberson, tried—though not always successfully—to avoid using the habitual term "nigger" while extending himself to be helpful to an inquiring black writer from New York. A member of the Martin County Historical Society, Manning was one of the sponsors of McCallum's above-cited invaluable history of that county during the Civil War.

16. Vincent Colyer, *Brief Report of the Services Rendered by the Freed People to the United States Army in North Carolina, in the Spring of 1862, After the Battle of Newbern* (New York: Vincent Colyer, 1864), p. 6.

17. Interview with Vernon Roberson at Robersonville, N.C., October 21,

1972. Roberson, a retired tobacco warehouseman and son of Joseph Alonzo Roberson, recalled having a close association with his grandfather Ezekiel, who was born around 1840 and died in the 1920s.

18. *Report of Persons and Articles Hired, Newberne, N.C.,* by Captain William Holden, File No. 516, Old Military Records Archive. William "Roberson" is listed in Vol. I, January–March 1863, Line 370; Vol. II, April, Line 434; Vol. III, May, Line 449, and June, Line 518. The sheets within each volume are unnumbered, and line numbers may be repeated on sheets other than those cited.

19. Vincent Colyer, *Brief Report of the Services Rendered,* pp. 9–10. Vincent Colyer of Brooklyn, N.Y., was appointed to the Union Army on March 10, 1862, as "Superintendent of the Poor for the Army of North Carolina," and was empowered to hire as many as 5,000 blacks at New Bern. Pertinent information on the subject is given by Benjamin Quarles, cited above.

20. A biography by Dorothy Gilliam, published five months after Robeson's death, asserted that having escaped from slavery prior to the Civil War, William Robeson in 1861 "joined the legions of other blacks fighting in the Union Army." (*Paul Robeson* [Washington, D.C.: New Republic Book Co., 1976], p. 4.) Blacks were not permitted to enlist until the latter part of 1862. Neither Paul Robeson nor his sister Marian ever heard their father mention having served in the army. Furthermore, an examination by the present writer of the service records in the Old Military Archives in Washington of seven black Union Army veterans named William Robeson (or variant spellings) disclosed that because of differences in age, parentage, birthplace, or length of service none was the William Robeson of this account.

21. Oliver O. Howard, *Autobiography of Oliver O. Howard, Major General, United States Army* (2 vols.; New York: Baker and Taylor, 1907), Vol. II, p. 177.

22. *Report of Persons and Articles Hired, New Berne, N.C., January–April, 1865,* by Captain A. S. Kimball. The cited entry is on line 295 on an unnumbered page headed, "Skilled Laborers."

23. Federal Census of 1870, enumerated on September 3, at Williamston Township, Martin County, N.C., p. 70, lines 15–23.

24. Federal Census of 1880, enumerated on June 3, at Cross Roads Township (a subdivision of the original Williamston Township), Martin County, N.C., p. 5, lines 4–6.

25. Martin County Courthouse, Williamston, N.C. The record of that license erroneously gives the age of Benjamin Congleton as sixty-seven.

26. Federal Census of 1870, Lower Oxford Township, Chester County, Pa., p. 36, line 6.

27. John Hope Franklin, *From Slavery to Freedom,* p. 276.

28. Lincoln University Catalogue, 1867–1868, p. 12.

29. Chester Valley, a post office from 1857 to 1906, was located near the town of Paoli, in Chester County, Pa. In later years at Lincoln University, William Robeson's residence was given as Warren Tavern, Pa., a post office from 1820 to

1910 that was located north of the present Borough of Malvern, also in Chester County.

30. Lincoln University Catalogue, 16th Annual Edition, p. 15.

31. *Ibid.,* 17th Annual Edition, p. 14.

32. *Oxford* [Pa.] *Press,* June 25, 1873.

33. Paul Robeson, *Here I Stand,* p. 26.

34. Lincoln University Catalogue, 1874–1875, p. 25.

35. *Local Daily News,* West Chester, Pa., October 31, 1876.

36. *Oxford* [Pa.] *Press,* June 14, 1876.

CHAPTER THREE

1. *Princeton Press,* April 9, 1898. (On microfilm at Princeton University Library.)

2. The text of the news account and Ida B. Wells's statement in full are quoted in Herbert Aptheker, ed., *A Documentary History of the Negro People in the United States* (New York: Citadel Press, 1951), Vol. II, p. 798.

3. *Princeton City Directory,* 1896. (At Princeton Historical Society.)

4. *Princeton Press,* July 2, 1898. All pupils in attendance were listed in the report of the school's closing exercises held on June 30 at the Witherspoon Street Presbyterian Church.

5. Anna Bustill Smith, *Reminiscences of Colored People of Princeton, N.J., 1800–1900* (a 16-page booklet, probably published by the author, c. 1913). (On microfilm at the Rutgers University Library.)

6. *Princeton Press,* July 8, 1899.

7. *Ibid.,* March 24, 1906.

8. Arthur S. Link, ed., *The First Presbyterian Church of Princeton* (Princeton: First Presbyterian Church, 1967), pp. 34–35.

9. "History of the Witherspoon Street Presbyterian Church," in the church directory of 1966–1967. No reference was made therein to the twenty-one-year pastorate of the Reverend William D. Robeson, by far the longest in the church's history; and though several of the memorial windows were mentioned, there was no reference to the window Rev. Robeson dedicated to his mother, Sabra.

10. *Princeton Press,* May 17, 1879. The paper recalled that the then-deceased Dr. James W. Alexander (whose views on the exclusion of the black members from his church were cited) "used to go down to Witherspoon Street, to that church carved out of ebony. He spent several years there." (Until the black church won the right to administer communion to its members, Dr. Alexander performed that service for them.)

11. *Ibid.,* October 1, 1881. The published excerpt of this sermon is the earliest expression of William D. Robeson that has been found.

12. *Ibid.,* December 3, 1898.

13. *Ibid.,* June 23, 1900.

14. *Ibid.,* October 13, 1900.

15. *Ibid.,* November 10, 1900.

16. *Ibid.,* November 17, 1900.

17. *Ibid.,* February 2, 1901.

18. Paul Robeson, "Here's My Story," *Freedom,* Vol. II, No. 4, April 1952, p. 5.

19. *Princeton Press,* February 16, 1901.

20. Paul Robeson, *Here I Stand,* p. 20.

21. Interview with Mrs. Virginia Rhetta, Chicago, April 17, 1972.

22. Paul Robeson, *Freedom,* April 1952, p. 1.

CHAPTER FOUR

1. Paul Robeson, *Here I Stand,* p. 23.

2. Paul Robeson, "Here's My Story," p. 5.

3. Paul Robeson, *Here I Stand,* p. 17.

4. *Ibid.,* p. 21.

5. William D. Robeson's change of denominations was effected on April 11, 1906. (Letter from Gerald W. Gillette, Research Historian, Presbyterian Historical Society, Philadelphia, December 16, 1971.)

6. *Princeton Press,* February 16, 1901.

7. Paul Robeson, "Here's My Story," p. 5.

8. Interview with Benjamin F. Gordon, New York, June 16, 1971.

9. *Princeton Press,* February 16, 1901.

10. Interview with Mrs. Marian Forsythe, Philadelphia, August 13, 1971.

11. Benjamin C. Robeson, "My Brother Paul," in *Here I Stand,* Appendix A, p. 120.

12. Interview of Paul Robeson by Pearl Bradley, March 21, 1944.

13. *Somerset Democrat,* Somerville, N.J., June 30, 1911.

14. Interview with Mrs. Margaret (Potter) Gibbons, New York, March 9, 1970.

CHAPTER FIVE

1. Interview with J. Douglas Brown, Princeton, N.J., December 4, 1969.

2. Interview with Stanley M. Douglas, New York, April 1, 1970. Mr. Douglas was an assistant attorney general of the State of New York for over twenty years. His first wife, Margaret Douglas, a New York City school official, was a cousin of Eslanda Goode Robeson, Paul Robeson's wife.

3. *The Valkyrie,* Somerville, N.J., June 1913.

4. Paul Robeson interview with Pearl Bradley, March 21, 1944.

5. Muriel Freeman, *Somerset Messenger-Gazette,* Somerville, N.J., April 19, 1973.

6. Interview with Samuel Woldin, Somerville, N.J., July 8, 1971.

7. Dorothy Sterling, ed., *Speak Out in Thunder Tones* (New York: Doubleday, 1973), p. 97.

8. Paul Robeson, *Here I Stand*, pp. 28–29.

9. From an address by J. Douglas Brown at a celebration of Paul Robeson's seventy-fifth birthday, Somerville, N.J., April 23, 1973.

10. Paul Robeson, *Here I Stand*, p. 19.

11. Interview with Mrs. Margaret (Potter) Gibbons, March 9, 1970.

12. Paul Robeson, *Here I Stand*, pp. 32–33.

13. The achievement was noted in two articles Robeson pasted into his college scrapbook—"The Dusky Rover," in *Outing* magazine, January 1918; and "Men of the Month," in *The Crisis*, Vol. XV, No. 5, March 1918, p. 229. The first article reported that he had "passed the examination with the highest average ever had in this competition," and the second asserted that "he made the highest average in the state," without specifying whether it was the highest ever.

14. Wendell Phillips, *Speeches, Lectures and Letters* (Boston: James Redpath, 1863), pp. 493–494.

15. Paul Robeson, *Here I Stand*, p. 8.

16. Elijah P. Lovejoy's open letter appeared November 5, 1835, in *The Observer*, a weekly Presbyterian paper he edited in St. Louis, Mo. The following year Rev. Lovejoy was compelled to move to Alton, Ill., where he published another antislavery paper until he was killed in 1837.

CHAPTER SIX

1. "Statement of the President with Report of the Dean and Report of the Librarian, Rutgers College, 1919–1920," p. 9. Seen at the Trenton State Library.

2. Robert Van Gelder, *New York Times*, January 16, 1944, Section 2, p. 7.

3. Montague Cobb, M.D., "Nathan Francis Mossell, M.D., 1856–1946," *Journal of the National Medical Association*, March 1954, Vol. VIL, No. 2, p. 122.

4. Interview with Harry J. Rockafeller at Rutgers University, New Brunswick, N.J., December 7, 1971.

5. Interview with Kenneth M. Rendell, Highland Park, N.J., December 7, 1971.

6. Interview with Alfred A. Neuschaefer, Trenton, N.J., December 7, 1971.

7. Interview with William A. Feitner, Montclair, N.J., January 26, 1972.

8. Interview with George F. Sanford Jr., New York, N.Y., January 31, 1972.

9. Letter to the author, November 14, 1971.

10. Letter to the author, February 18, 1972.

11. Alice M. Bacon, *The Negro and the Atlanta Exposition* (Baltimore: Trustees of the Slater Fund, 1896), p. 15. The text of Booker T. Washington's historic speech at Atlanta on September 18, 1895, has since been reprinted in numerous anthologies.

12. Shirley Graham, *Paul Robeson, Citizen of the World*, p. 83.

13. Letter to the author, January 22, 1973.

14. The information in the footnote is from Herbert Aptheker, ed., *Documentary History*, Vol. II, p. 583.

15. Letter to the author, February 24, 1972.

16. James D. Carr, letter to Rutgers president William H. S. Demarest, June 6, 1919. In Special Collections, Rutgers University Library, New Brunswick, N.J.

17. Interview with Frederick B. Pollard, New York, N.Y., July 8, 1970.

CHAPTER SEVEN

1. New Brunswick *Daily Home News*, April 24, 1918.

2. D. L. Reeves, "Rutgers Team a Powerful Unit of Speed and Brawn; Robeson the Most Versatile Player of the Age," *Philadelphia Public Ledger*, November 10, 1918.

3. Robert W. Maxwell, "Rutgers Lives Up to 'Rep' and Hands Lehigh a Beating," *Public Ledger* [?], 1918. Scrapbook clipping.

4. *Rutgers Alumni Quarterly*, January 1918, Vol. IV, No. 2, p. 75.

5. Lawrence Perry, "Why Does a Winner Win?" *Association Men of Y.M.C.A.*, Vol. XLV, No. 6, February 1924, p. 248.

6. "Naval Team Fails to Check Rutgers," *New York Times*, November 6, 1918.

7. The official at the Rutgers 40-0 victory over Naval Transport of Hoboken in 1918 was Tom Thorp, who was also a sports writer for the *New York Sun*. (Unidentified scrapbook clipping.)

8. *Rutgers Alumni Quarterly*, January 1918, Vol. IV, No. 2, p. 75.

9. Frederick G. Lieb, "Rutgers Football Legions Overthrow Fordham Team," *New York Sun*, October 28, 1917.

10. Charles A. Taylor, "Maroon Grid Warriors Smothered by Rutgers," *New York Tribune*, October 28, 1917.

11. "Fordham Crushed by Rutgers Power," *New York Times*, October 28, 1917.

12. Louis Lee Arms, "Rutgers Blanks Navy," *New York Sunday Tribune*, November 25, 1917.

13. George Daley, "Robeson Takes a Place with Elect of Football," *New York World*, November 28, 1917.

14. *Rutgers Alumni Quarterly*, January 1918, Vol. IV, No. 2, p. 75.

15. Walter Camp, "War and Football," *Collier's Weekly*, January 15, 1918, p. 32.

16. *Ibid.*

17. *Ibid.*, p. 47.

18. Paul Robeson, "Review of the 1917 Football Season," *Rutgers Alumni Quarterly*, January 1918, Vol. IV., No. 1, pp. 69–75.

19. *Targum*, March 16, 1918, Vol. 49, No. 19.

20. *The Crisis*, March 1918, Vol. XV, No. 5, pp. 229–231.

21. *Ibid.*, March 1919, Vol. XVII, No. 5, pp. 233–234.

22. *The Scarlet Letter, 1919.* [Actually 1918. The Rutgers yearbooks were confusingly dated. Thus the "1919" number was issued in 1918, when Robeson's Class of 1919 was completing its junior year.]

CHAPTER EIGHT

1. Interview with Mrs. Margaret (Potter) Gibbons, March 9, 1970.

2. Somerville, N.J., *Unionist Gazette,* May 23, 1918.

3. The printed program for the family reunion held on June 21, 1918, at Maple Grove in Philadelphia listed the following persons as officers of the Bustill Family Association: James Bustill Jones, president; Mrs. Gertrude Bustill Mossell, first vice president; Charles Bustill Jones, second vice president; Dr. A. T. Boyer, secretary; Miss Arabella Pierce, assistant secretary; and Mrs. I. Bowser Asbury, treasurer. Dr. Boyer and Miss Pierce were also shown as members of the executive committee, together with Mrs. Mary L. De Coursey, Mrs. Charles Bustill Jones, Mrs. Mary Mossell Griffin, Mrs. Elsie Newsome, and Mrs. Ella E. Lyons.

4. Paul Robeson, *Here I Stand,* p. 16.

5. Interview with Mrs. Christine Moore Howell, New Brunswick, N.J., January 27, 1972.

6. Mrs. Virginia Bustill Rhetta, daughter of the Bustill family historian Anna Bustill Smith, had a copy of the program of the Bustill reunion held at Gouldtown, N.J., on September 5, 1938. It is not known if the annual gatherings were continued after that year.

7. The quotation in the footnote is from Eslanda Goode Robeson, *Paul Robeson, Negro,* p. 23.

8. The record of the Rutgers football team on which Robeson played was as follows (Rutgers scores are given first):

1915—Won 7, Lost 1, Tied 0: Albright, 54-0; Princeton, 0-10; Renssalaer, 96-0; Muhlenberg, 21-0; Springfield YMCA, 44-13; All Stars, 28-7; Stevens, 39-3; New York University, 70-0.

1916—Won 3, Lost 2, Tied 2: Villanova, 30-0; Washington and Lee, 13-13; Brown, 3-21; Holy Cross, 14-7; West Virginia, 0-0; Dickinson, 34-0; Washington and Jefferson, 9-12.

1917—Won 7, Lost 1, Tied 1: Ursinus, 25-0; Fort Wadsworth, 96-0; Syracuse, 10-14; Lafayette, 33-7; Fordham, 28-0; West Virginia, 7-7; Springfield, 61-0; League Island Marines, 27-0; Newport Naval Reserves, 14-0.

1918—Won 5, Lost 2, Tied 0: Ursinus, 66-0; Pelham Bay Naval, 7-0; Lehigh, 39-0; Naval Transport of Hoboken, 40-0; Penn State, 26-0; Great Lakes Naval Training Station, 14-54; Syracuse, 0-20.

9. January 4, 1919, pp. 13, 62.

10. W. J. Baird, New Brunswick *Daily Home News,* October 23, 1918.

11. *Ibid.,* undated 1918 scrapbook clipping.

12. Hilton S. Read, "Robeson Played Best Game of His Career in Last Attempt to Beat Princeton," *Daily Home News*, undated 1919 scrapbook clipping.

13. "Robeson Wins Extemporaneous Speaking Contest," *Targum*, April 30, 1919.

14. The quotation in the footnote is from Madison, Wisconsin, *Capital Times*, December 11, 1929.

15. *Targum*, June 1919, pp. 570–572.

16. *Daily Home News*, June 11, 1919.

17. June 15, 1919, Section II, p. 4.

18. *Targum*, June 1919, p. 566.

CHAPTER NINE

1. New Brunswick *Daily Home News*, June 5, 1919.

2. John Hope Franklin, *From Slavery to Freedom*, p. 480.

3. *Ibid.*

4. *The Crisis*, August 1919, p. 191.

5. Paul Robeson, "The Fourteenth Amendment, 'The Sleeping Giant of the American Constitution,'" Senior thesis, Rutgers University, May 29, 1919.

6. *Congressional Record*, Vol. 58, Part 5. 66th Congress, 1st session (Washington, D.C.: U.S. Government Printing Office, August 5, 1919), p. 4305.

7. Walter R. Lofton, "Commencement Orators Tell of Dawn of New Day," unidentified scrapbook newspaper clipping. Dr. May E. Chinn, a New York physician, provided the author with a printed program of the evening, which listed her to follow Robeson's speech with several piano numbers.

CHAPTER TEN

1. Alain Locke, ed., *The New Negro* (New York: Albert and Charles Boni, 1925), p. 6.

2. Interview with May E. Chinn, M.D., New York, February 19, 1972.

3. Interview with Michael Harold Higgins, Bloomfield, N.J., March 13, 1972.

4. Letter to the author, March 26, 1975.

5. George Foster Sanford Jr., message to Paul Robeson, recorded by author, New York, January 31, 1972.

6. Interview with Milton J. Rettenberg, New York, March 10, 1975.

7. Undated scrapbook clipping.

8. Lloyd Larson, "Badger Pros Capture First Home Game from Racine, 20-0." Undated clipping.

9. "Badgers Trim Thorpe's Team." Undated clipping.

10. Interview with Pearl M. Fisher and Mrs. Jane Fisher, sister and widow, respectively, of Rudolph Fisher, October 12, 1971.

CHAPTER ELEVEN

1. Interview with Frederick B. (Fritz) Pollard, New York, June 8, 1970.
2. Maida Castellun, "The Stage," New York *Call,* April 7, 1922.
3. Interview with British Broadcasting Corporation, London, 1958. In recalling the incident Robeson mistakenly identified the play in which he was appearing as *The Emperor Jones.*
4. Interview with Lawrence Brown, New York, August 8, 1971.
5. A definitive review of Robeson's artistic career is given in *Paul Robeson: His Career in the Theatre, in Motion Pictures, and on the Concert Stage,* by Anatol I. Schlosser (Doctoral dissertation, New York University, 1970).
6. Paul Robeson, *Here I Stand,* p. 49.
7. Paul Robeson, "An Actor's Wanderings and Hopes," *The Messinger,* January 1925, p. 32. A. Philip Randolph, then a socialist, was coeditor of that self-styled "radical magazine." He later founded and led the Brotherhood of Sleeping Car Porters.
8. Interview with Walter Abel, Bedford Hills, N.Y., July 30, 1971.
9. Paul Robeson, *Here I Stand,* p. 53.

AFTERWORD

1. *Lift Every Voice for Paul Robeson* (New York: Freedom Associates, 1951). The cover drawing by Hugo Gellert depicted Robeson as Gulliver, standing tall while tethered by Lilliputians, and in the background there is a weeping Statue of Liberty.
2. *Iron City* (New York: Masses & Mainstream, 1951; reprinted Boston: Northeastern University Press, 1994).
3. Paul Robeson, "The Brave Trumpets of Albert Einstein and His Fellow Scientists," *Freedom,* November 1952.
4. Richard Alan Schwartz, "The F.B.I. and Albert Einstein," *The Nation,* September 3–10, 1983, p. 168.
5. Philip Foner, ed., *Paul Robeson Speaks* (New York: Bruner/Mazel, 1978), p. 173.
6. Full text in *Here I Stand,* pp. 119–121.
7. The author has a tape recording of Robeson's speech at the Hotel Americana, New York, April 22, 1965.
8. Craig R. Watson, *Courier-Post,* Camden, N.J., July 25, 1970, pp. 3–5.
9. Paul Robeson, *Here I Stand,* p. 14.
10. "Ten Greats of Black History," *Ebony,* August 1972, pp. 35–42. Listed here in the order of their births, the ten were: Richard Allen, (1769), Nat Turner (1800), Frederick Douglass (1817), Booker T. Washington (1865) W.E.B. Du Bois (1868), Marcus Garvey (1887), Paul Robeson (1898), Thurgood Marshall

(1908), Malcolm X (1925), and Martin Luther King Jr. (1929). Robeson and Marshall were the only ones still living.

11. The tape recordings are held by the author.

12. Laurie Johnston, "Robeson, at 75, Is Feted in Absentia," April 16, 1973.

APPENDIX A

1. Henry H. Bisbee, *Place Names in Burlington County, New Jersey* (Riverside, N.J.: Burlington County Publishing Co., 1955), p. 21.

2. Benjamin Franklin, *The Autobiography of Benjamin Franklin,* ed. Leonard W. Labaree (New Haven: Yale University Press, 1964), pp. 112–113.

3. The statement is quoted in full in Herbert Aptheker, *And Why Not Every Man?* (New York: International, 1970), pp. 28–30.

4. Anna Bustill Smith, "The Bustill Family," *Journal of Negro History,* Vol. X, No. 4, October 1925, pp. 638–647.

5. Virginia Bustill Smith Rhetta, "The Bustill Family" (unpublished manuscript, n.d.), p. 1.

6. The original will is in the Archives and History Bureau, New Jersey State Library.

7. Virginia Bustill Smith Rhetta, "The Bustill Family." This account varies considerably from an earlier narrative that has Cyrus Bustill starting to learn the baking trade in 1762 (when he was thirty) and becoming a journeyman seven years later—a circumstance that might explain his late marriage at age forty-one. The version giving the later apprenticeship was found in an undated clipping from a periodical of the United Order of Odd Fellows that serialized the Bustill history to 1887. That narrative was probably written by Mrs. Rhetta's grandfather, Joseph C. Bustill, a leading member of the Odd Fellows, a fraternal organization founded by free blacks in 1843.

8. From undated clippings of an account of the Bustills to 1887. (See the preceding note concerning that publication.)

9. Anna Bustill Smith, "The Bustill Family," p. 639.

10. *Ibid.,* p. 638.

11. Herbert Aptheker, *The Negro in the Abolitionist Movement* (New York: International, 1941), p. 30.

12. William Douglass, *Annals of the First African Church* (Philadelphia: King and Baird Printers, 1862), p. 52.

13. Anna Bustill Smith, "The Bustill Family," p. 643.

14. Letter to William Bassett, December 1837, in G. H. Barnes and D. L. Dumond, eds., *Letters of Theodore Dwight Weld, Angelina Grimké Weld, and Sarah Grimké, 1822–1844* (2 vols., New York: D. Appleton-Century, 1934), Vol. II, p. 830.

15. *Ibid.,* p. 831.

16. *Ibid.*, pp. 792–793. Letter from Sarah M. Grimké to Elizabeth Pease.

17. Anna Bustill Smith, "The Bustill Family," p. 640.

18. *Ibid.*

19. *The Liberator,* April 10, 1857.

20. William Still, *The Underground Rail Road,* pp. 611–612.

21. *Ibid.,* p. 43.

22. *Ibid.,* p. 218.

23. *Ibid.,* p. 221.

24. Anna Bustill Smith, "The Bustill Family," p. 641.

25. Virginia Bustill Smith Rhetta, "The Bustill Family," p. 2.

26. West Chester, Pa., *Local Daily News,* October 31, 1876. Original clipping at Chester County Historical Society.

27. Mrs. N. F. Mossell, *The Work of the Afro-American Woman* (Philadelphia: Geo. S. Ferguson, 1894).

28. Montague Cobb, M.D., "Nathan Francis Mossell, M.D., 1856–1946," p. 120.

About the Book and Author

Famous as a football star and prizewinning student, then acclaimed as a world-class concert singer and actor on stage and screen, Paul Robeson became one of America's most controversial figures during the Cold War. Hailed by many as a forerunner of the civil rights movement, he was denounced by others and seen by the U.S. government as a threat to the nation's security at home and abroad.

Now for the first time there is an illuminating, firsthand view of this remarkable African American by a writer who is uniquely qualified to tell the story. A close friend and coworker of Robeson's for over thirty years, Lloyd L. Brown assisted in the writing of Robeson's book *Here I Stand*. Now he has combined painstaking research with personal observation in his own book, *The Young Paul Robeson*. He brings to the work a graceful and engaging literary style developed over his many years as an essayist and critic on African American literature and culture.

Reflecting on interviews with Robeson's schoolmates in elementary school, high school, Rutgers University, and Columbia Law School and drawing on original information from other sources, Brown provides a well-paced narrative of Robeson's life from his birth in Princeton to the budding of his artistic career in Harlem. Because Robeson always attributed his achievements to the guiding hand of his slave-born father, the Reverend William D. Robeson, Brown traced Robeson's ancestral roots to North Carolina, where he found and interviewed cousins of Robeson as well as descendants of the family that had owned Robeson's father and his grandparents. Brown's discovery of how William Robeson escaped to freedom and gained academic excellence is one of the many aspects of the Paul Robeson legend told here for the first time.

Lloyd L. Brown, an Afro-American writer and former editor, is the author of the novel *Iron City*.

Index